The Godfather of Gore Speaks

Herschell Gordon Lewis Discusses His Films

by
Herschell Gordon Lewis
with
Andrew J. Rausch

Foreword by
Christopher Wayne Curry

Introduction by
Mike White

The Godfather of Gore Speaks
© 2012 Herschell Gordon Lewis and Andrew J. Rausch
All rights reserved.

No portion of this publication may be reproduced, stored, and/or copied electronically (except for academic use as a source), nor transmitted in any form or by any means without the prior written permission of the publisher and/or author(s).

Published in the USA by:
BearManor Media
P.O. Box 1129
Duncan, OK 73534-1129
www.BearManorMedia.com

ISBN: 1-59393-297-9
ISBN-13: 978-1-59393-297-8

Printed in the United States

Design and Layout by Scot Penslar.
Photographs appear courtesy of Christopher Wayne Curry.

"If you live long enough, you become legitimate. Some of the comments that I hear today are totally out of sync with the comments I heard when we first made these movies. At the time, I suppose I was regarded as an outlaw in the movie business. 'Who is this screwball who isn't even in California? And who's grinding out this stuff like so much hamburger?'"

— Herschell Gordon Lewis

In memory of

David F. Friedman

CONTENTS

FOREWORD *by Christopher Wayne Curry* .5

INTRODUCTION *by Mike White* 7

CHAPTER 1 9
The Prime Time – Living Venus – The Adventures of Lucky Pierre

CHAPTER 2 25
*Daughter of the Sun – Nature's Playmates –
Goldilocks and the Three Bares*

CHAPTER 3 35
Boin-n-g! – Scum of the Earth – Bell, Bare and Beautiful

CHAPTER 4 47
Blood Feast – Two Thousand Maniacs! – Color Me Blood Red

CHAPTER 5 65
Moonshine Mountain – Monster A-Go-Go – Sin, Suffer, and Repent

CHAPTER 6 77
*An Eye for an Eye – Jimmy the Boy Wonder –
The Magic Land of Mother Goose*

CHAPTER 7 83
Something Weird – Suburban Roulette – Blast-Off Girls

CHAPTER 8 91
*The Girl, the Body, and the Pill – A Taste of Blood –
The Gruesome Twosome*

CHAPTER 9 101
Alley Tramp – She-Devils on Wheels – Just for the Hell of It

CHAPTER 10 109
The Psychic – How to Make a Doll – The Ecstasies of Women

CHAPTER 11 115
Linda and Abilene – The Wizard of Gore – Miss Nymphet's Zap-In

CHAPTER 12 123
Black Love – This Stuff'll Kill Ya! – Year of the Yahoo!

CHAPTER 13 129
The Gore Gore Girls – Blood Feast 2: All U Can Eat – The Uh! Oh! Show

FOREWORD
by Christopher Wayne Curry

In 1963, Herschell Gordon Lewis managed to change the face of horror cinema forever. He armed himself with his latest production — a cheap, bare bones, bloody mess of a movie entitled *Blood Feast*. Twenty-odd years later, after the fact, Herschell's low-rent calling card (still an unusual and ghastly sight to endure) forever changed how I would face cinema in general.

Once I'd stumbled upon Herschell's peculiar brand of movie-making, all other filmmakers and films were suspect. Having spent my previous years steeped in big and bloated Hollywood productions I found Herschell's penny-pinching talents refreshing, and there was a lesson to be learned in them.

The direction of *Blood Feast* is stilted. The acting is stiff. The pacing is slow and the script is chock full of impossibilities, but none of that makes a damned bit of difference. Herschell's maiden voyage into a sea of blood was nothing short of incredibly entertaining, and that is what good cinema is all about.

So much of American horror remained rooted in the Gothic. Even Hitchcock's *Psycho* (realized a mere three years later) has a Victorian-looking mansion at its center. But Herschell sliced and diced and literally ripped away those horror confines. He brought the horror home. He brought it closer to a contemporary reality, and if you happened to live anywhere near the Suez Motel in Miami, Florida, Herschell's razor-sharp point was driven straight into the heart of your home, your reality.

Now that's a lesson for filmmakers. Break away from the norm. Break away from the form. Whether by design or a crippling monetary budget (it doesn't matter how he got there, just be glad that he did), *Blood Feast* became the first of its kind. It made Herschell a boatload of cash and put his name in the cinema history books. In fact, you're holding the fourth book to be authored on the Mad Hatter of Splatter.

Was there anything particularly poignant or thought-provoking in an H.G. Lewis production? Not thematically, no. But what is there is a sort of cinematic time capsule.

Herschell was able to capture the actual dress and hair styles of the average American in the 1960s and early '70s. He did the same with the restaurants, nightclubs, hotel rooms, and homes. These were actual representations of people and places at the exact time of filming, and for Herschell that usually meant South Florida or Chicago. Obviously budget constraints dictated that existing locations be utilized rather than the construction of sets, but the overall effect is unique when compared to a Hollywood production where almost nothing is "real."

So, the big lesson here is that a large budget doesn't necessarily make for an entertaining movie. Some Hollywood movies (and I won't name names) have enough scratch in them to help balance the U.S. budget and they're either laughable or simply unwatchable. Each and every one of Herschell's films are enjoyable on some front.

Herschell not only invented the genre of gore, he also created a number of "nudie cuties," the first "roughie" (*Scum of the Earth*), and managed to advance his filmmaking trek into wife-swapping and ESP to rock-and-roll to LSD. Thirty-seven movies in all, and in just 12 short years. Then Herschell retired from filmmaking for good, or so he thought.

Since Herschell has reemerged as a movie-maker, he has officially been twisting and deforming the face of cinema for over 50 years, and for that I am glad.

Christopher Wayne Curry is the author of the books A Taste of Blood: The Films of Herschell Gordon Lewis *(Creation Books, 1999) and* Film Alchemy: The Independent Cinema of Ted V. Mikels *(McFarland & Company, Inc., 2007).*

INTRODUCTION
by Mike White

It's a joy to hear Herschell Gordon Lewis talk to an audience. He's got a natural ability to tell stories. It took me years to find out, but I'm a part of one of his oft-told tales but definitely not the star of it.

A few years ago, I attended the Cinema Wasteland convention in Cleveland just to see Mr. Lewis and his latest film, *The Uh! Oh! Show*. He took questions after the film and started relating a story about being in Baltimore years before where one of the other people on the same panel (Brian Horrorwitz of *Trash Palace* fame) tried to impress Mr. Lewis by pretending to pull out his own eye. That would have been good for a little bit of a chuckle except that Brian managed to get a good deal of stage blood on Mr. Lewis's khakis, the only clean pair he had packed.

I sat anonymously in the audience at Cinema Wasteland, listening to the story and laughing to myself to hear it retold all those years later. I had been sitting next to Mr. Lewis as the moderator of the panel and heard about his pants for the next few hours as the story passed around the lobby of the Charles Theater.

Not all brushes with greatness are so great. To be honest, I'm glad that Mr. Lewis doesn't remember me from that experience. I'd rather not be associated with his bloody pants.

What has always impressed me about Herschell Gordon Lewis is the way he anticipated, led, or created trends in cinema. He broke new ground with the "nudie cutie" films, directing the first nudie musical, *Goldilocks and the Three Bares*. He created the first entry in the "roughie" subgenre with *Scum of the Earth*. And, of course, he opened the door to gore with *Blood Feast*. For better or for worse, we'd not have directors like Eli Roth or Gaspar Noé had we not had characters like Fuad Ramses.

In *The Uh! Oh! Show*, Mr. Lewis plays Uncle Herschell, and that's kind of the role I always picture him playing in real life. Or, better yet, he's like the grandfather you've never had but always wanted. Sure, gramps might seem respectable but he's got this wealth of stories about a mysterious past that grandma doesn't like him to talk about.

In *The Godfather of Gore Speaks*, Andrew Rausch combines Herschell Gordon Lewis's storytelling ability and the tales behind how Lewis came to direct some of the most groundbreaking films in cinema history. With this book, readers will be able to glean what makes this true independent filmmaker and honest-to-goodness auteur tick.

Now, pull up a chair, relax, and listen to Uncle Herschell.

Mike White is a gadfly from Detroit who's tried to make a name for himself editing and publishing the indie film 'zine Cashiers du Cinemart. *He can also be heard on the weekly film podcast The Projection Booth.*

NOTE TO READERS:

For clarity, all of Herschell Gordon Lewis' words are in this typeface.

Andrew J. Rausch's running commentary is in this typeface and is set apart from the main text in this manner.

The Prime Time - Living Venus - The Adventures of Lucky Pierre

"I don't want The Prime Time *on my epitaph because I found out that the producer is really just somebody who puts up the money. I found that I didn't function well as an outsider. I guess it was because after working all those years and having learned all the technical tricks, I could really, at the time, make a movie all alone."*

— Herschell Gordon Lewis

The genesis of *The Prime Time*, Herschell Gordon Lewis' first foray into feature filmmaking, was a simple conversation in which someone asked him why he didn't make features. Lewis found that he had no good answer for this question. He had already worked extensively in radio and television and was currently making commercials and industrial films, so the idea of making a feature film was not without merit.

This inspired Lewis to make a film, so he hired a screenwriter to craft a script. He then pitched his film idea to Chicago's Modern Film Distributors with his future partner-in-crime, producer David F. Friedman, present. Rather than giving the standard speech about wanting to make the greatest film ever produced, the practical Lewis simply explained that he wanted to make a film that would make money. Lewis' no-nonsense pitch won over the savvy businessmen and they agreed to distribute the picture.

Lewis, ever the showman, decided to have a contest that allowed newspaper readers to suggest possible titles for the film. The filmmaker received nearly 5,000 entries. The winners, twin brothers from Sarasota, Florida, suggested the title *The Prime Time* and won a $50 savings bond for the effort. Other notable promotions included best beard contests at theaters, as well as the release of a novelization and a soundtrack album which featured the songs "The Prime Time" and "Teenage Tiger." The film was released as the bottom half of a double bill with a re-release of Kurt Neumann's 1954 film *Carnival Story*.

Although *The Prime Time* would ultimately disappoint Lewis in terms of quality and profit, it is significant because its $100,000 budget would be the largest with which Lewis would work in his early career, and also because it launched the career of a young ingénue named Karen Black. Although the actress originally filmed a scene in which she appeared topless, her agent later paid the filmmaker $2,500 to destroy the footage before the film's completion. The film is also significant because it would be the last time Lewis worked on a film he didn't control.

Way, way back in the period between 1960, when we made *The Prime Time*, and 1974, when I quit making movies for a while, there was an odd but profitable period for independent filmmaking.

I operated a little commercial film studio in Chicago, which was originally called Lewis and Martin Films. My partner was a man named Martin Schmidhofer. Lewis and Schmidhofer would not have fit on the building, so we used my last name and his first. That might have been a benefit or might have been a curse, because at that time, Dean Martin and Jerry Lewis were a well-known comedy duo. People were always saying, "Is this Dean and Jerry?" Well, no, it wasn't. It was Herschell and Marty. But it made no difference to us, and off we went making films.

In the course of all this, I bought 35mm movie equipment — primarily to make commercials. However, the big advertising agencies paid no attention to a Chicago studio that had 35mm equipment. They simply went to the west coast to shoot their material. And this, of course, was prior to the days of videocassettes or any of the other contemporary techniques. So I was complaining one day to someone I hardly knew about my misfortunes in the movie business, and he said, "Well, how do you make any money in the movie business?" I said, "The only way to make money in the movie business is to make features." And he said, "So why don't you make features?" I said, "No one makes features in Chicago." He said, "Nonsense. Charlie Chaplin shot his first features at the Essanay studios right here in Chicago." Well, that started the saliva flowing. I then put together a company we called Mid-Continent Films, which was designed to make two features. As often happens during someone's invasion into an area in which he or she feels that they know everything, it quickly becomes apparent that he or she knows nothing.

Finding no difficulty at all in putting together a script, I hired someone to write one for me. I then hired a man named Gordon Weisenborn to direct the movie. In some filmographies, they say I used Gordon Weisenborn as a pseudonym on the picture. This was not the case. I assure you, Gordon Weisenborn was a real person. He worked for the Fred Niles Film Studio as a staff director. I had never even considered the possibility that someone who could photograph commercial subjects might not do as well filming drama.

At that point, someone brought up the question of distribution. On South Wabash Avenue, there was, at that time, an area known as Film Row. This was comprised of a number of independent film producers. That's long gone now. The independents have now either been absorbed into major companies, or their independent output is being distributed on a different basis altogether. I was recommended to one such company called Modern

Film Distributors. Film insiders told me, "This fellow is hardboiled, but he will get your picture out there and into theaters." At that time, it was theaters or nothing. Down I went to South Wabash Avenue to discuss my project, which would ultimately be called *The Prime Time*. At that meeting with this fellow, Erwin Joseph, who was indeed rather hard-bitten and treated me like the naïve young man that I was, was a young man who was his associate. His name was David Friedman. He and I hit it off immediately. But my relationship with Erwin Joseph was a different story altogether. We weren't quite at sword point, but I'd say we simply didn't care much for each other. But Dave and I immediately recognized some spark between the two of us. So I made a deal with Modern Film Distributors to handle the distribution of *The Prime Time* once the film was finished, which it was in short order.

The film was in black-and-white, and I made just about every mistake a beginner can make. First of all, I hired an outside director who had never previously shot a feature. Also, I made the mistake of having an I.A. crew. That's short for I.A.T.S.E., which stands for the International Alliance of Theatrical Stage Employees. They are a motion picture union, and they really stuck it to me. In Chicago, no one had shot a feature in years. I'm not even sure the I.A. even existed when Chaplin had filmed his movies there. So the production cost of *The Prime Time* was substantially more than it should have been. The plotline was a not a very good one either, but I didn't realize this until after the fact. This fellow Fred Niles, who owned the studio where Weisenborn worked, recommended the screenwriter, Robert Abel. I was told that Abel had written a script which had been a big success called *The Giant Behemoth* — a title which is a redundancy. I should have known that at the time, as well. (I might point out that I later learned claims that Abel had written *The Giant Behemoth* were completely false.) The resulting screenplay wasn't very good, and I knew it at the time. However, I was the lone dissenter here; everyone else thought the script was great, so I kept my mouth shut.

A scene from The Prime Time *featuring actress Karen Black in her screen debut.*

So off we went to shoot this movie. I remember one scene called for a Luigi's Restaurant. In order to save money, we actually found a restaurant in Chicago called Luigi's. And this fellow was absolutely thrilled that we were going to shoot a movie on his premises. The only problem was that he wouldn't shut down while we were filming. So we had to film this scene while the restaurant was open, and there were customers walking in front of the camera and spoiling takes. Customers would yell, "What are you guys doing?" right in the middle of the scene. We had this fellow named Herb Graham — he was an announcer in Chicago — and he was playing the waiter in Luigi's Restaurant. There was a scene in which the protagonist went into the restaurant, and the waiter was cleaning a table. Gordon Weisenborn tried to show the waiter what to do. At that point, one of the real waiters in the restaurant said, "That's not right!" He then ran over and showed Herb how to wipe off the top of the table.

The Prime Time would also be the first movie to feature a young actress named Karen Black. She was the girlfriend of a guy named Bill Erman, who was the brother of Dick Erman, one of my investors in Mid-Continent Films. Bill Erman wanted this creature who was a student at Northwestern University — a fact that had some hold on me since I had attended Northwestern University — to be in the movie. So we cast Karen Black. We were shooting at a hidden quarry, which doubled as a swimming pool, and Dave Friedman insisted that we have this one uncovered breast scene. Karen Black was supposed to do that scene. We were shooting that, and Bill Erman came rushing onto the set. "No, no," he said. "She's a star-to-be, and she can't do a scene topless!" And we were already shooting it, so we had to replace it with another scene shot at United Film and Recording.

And sure enough, once this movie was finished, between Erwin Joseph's connections and Dave Friedman's brashness, we got the movie to play in a number of places. I wasn't surprised. Being as naïve as I was, I expected it to make a big splash. I thought we might open at Radio City Music Hall. But all of this naïveté eventually washes away. Audience reactions were tepid, to say the least. A lot of people didn't understand why we made that movie, and eventually I had to join in the chorus, too. The script that Robert Abel had written was not dramatic at all. It was supposedly the coming to life of a young guy, but it didn't make a lot of sense. The gal who played the lead was named Jo Ann LeCompte, and she was married to a New York theatrical producer named Noel Behn. He made remarks that, at the time, I felt were insulting. He said, "There's no drama here." And of course he was right. But at the time we had made *The Prime Time*, I was really at the mercy of Fred Niles and the people he had recommended. That would be a bitter and expensive lesson for me that paid off long-term.

H.G. Lewis' second film, *Living Venus*, would mark his directorial debut. The film would tell the story of a publisher loosely based on *Playboy* magnate Hugh Hefner, who ultimately becomes a victim of his own success. Retaining complete control of the film this time out, Lewis would create a motion picture—arguably one of his finest—of which he could be proud. Unlike *The Prime Time*, this was a quality film that actually appealed to audiences.

Lewis and producer David Friedman would discover actor Bill Kerwin in a Catholic recruiting film. This would be the first of many Lewis/Kerwin collaborations. Once the filmmakers found their lead actor, they then discovered another actor who had appeared with Kerwin in an industrial film about meat carving. They found that the actor, a then unknown Harvey Korman (of *The Carol Burnett Show* fame), had terrific chemistry with Kerwin.

We made a second film, and this one was called *Living Venus*. I tried to correct all the mistakes I had made in making *The Prime Time*. First of all, I directed it myself. Second, I was much more careful in allowing the I.A. to dictate to me how big a crew I should have and exactly what each person's responsibility was. And third, I had a screenplay from a fellow named Jim McGinn, who actually knew how to write a script. *Living Venus* appealed to me because the dialogue was much more realistic and much more biting than the dialogue in *The Prime Time*. So I felt that this would be a picture that was much more playable.

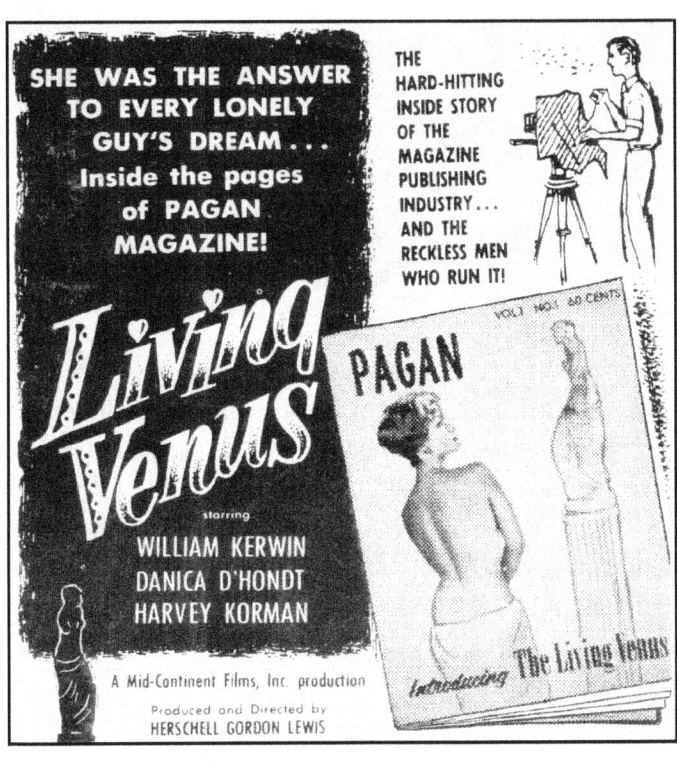

The film was to be about the rise and eventual fall of a character based loosely on Hugh Hefner, the guru of the *Playboy* empire. At that moment he was really at his height. I see he's now come back and almost married a 24-year-old girl and bought out his partners at *Playboy*, so he's still very much in the business. The idea of having him fall was really fictional, but the idea of the character was not fictional, and I felt at the time it was timely.

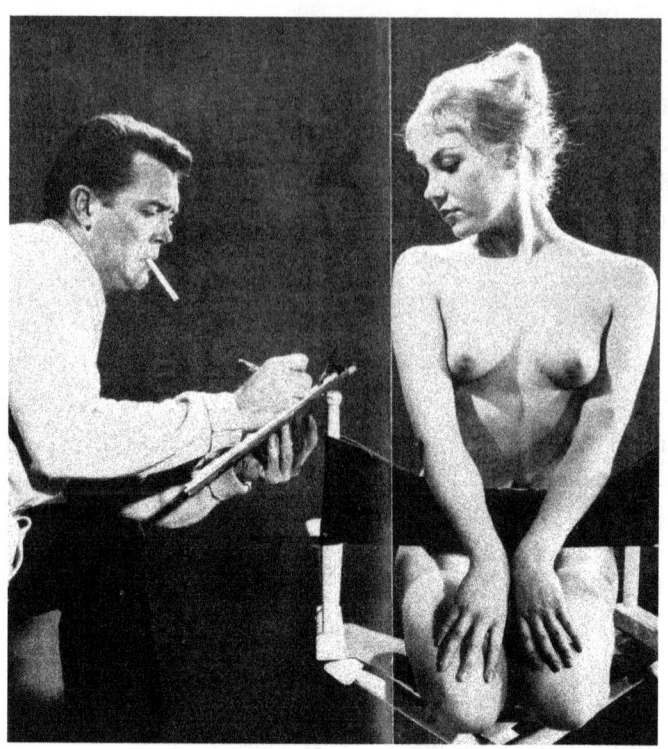

A scene from the film *Living Venus*.

Living Venus was the first film on which I worked with an actor named Bill Kerwin. He would ultimately become a staple in my films under pseudonyms like Rooney Kerwin and Thomas Sweetwood. I wouldn't call it a fierce competition for that role, but anyone involved in any kind of theatre in Chicago was aware that a movie had been made in Chicago and that the man who made that movie was now making a new one. So I was holding auditions for *Living Venus*, and there was a scene in which there was an argument between a man and his girlfriend. They were lined up, and it never occurred to me to have privacy for these auditions. People were watching others auditioning for the same role. One of these guys who was auditioning for the lead role slapped this girl who was supposed to be his girlfriend. It called for a slap, but he actually hit her, and she staggered backwards. We were all apologizing to her — including him. He didn't get the part, by the way. But when Bill Kerwin came up, he asked her, "Should I slap you?" And she said, "If you do, I'll slap you back, whether it's in the script or not!"

Once casting was finished, we began filming. I rushed *Living Venus* to completion. We cut it at a place called United Film and Recording Studio. By that time, I had had all I could take of the Fred Niles Studio. So I had a little more independence and a little more authority than I had previously on *The Prime Time*.

While shooting scenes with Danica D'Hondt, the girl who played Venus, I learned another valuable lesson. She brought her agent with her to the set, and I quickly learned not to deal with actors who have agents. You can't do it when you are working in the budgetary arena that I'm in.

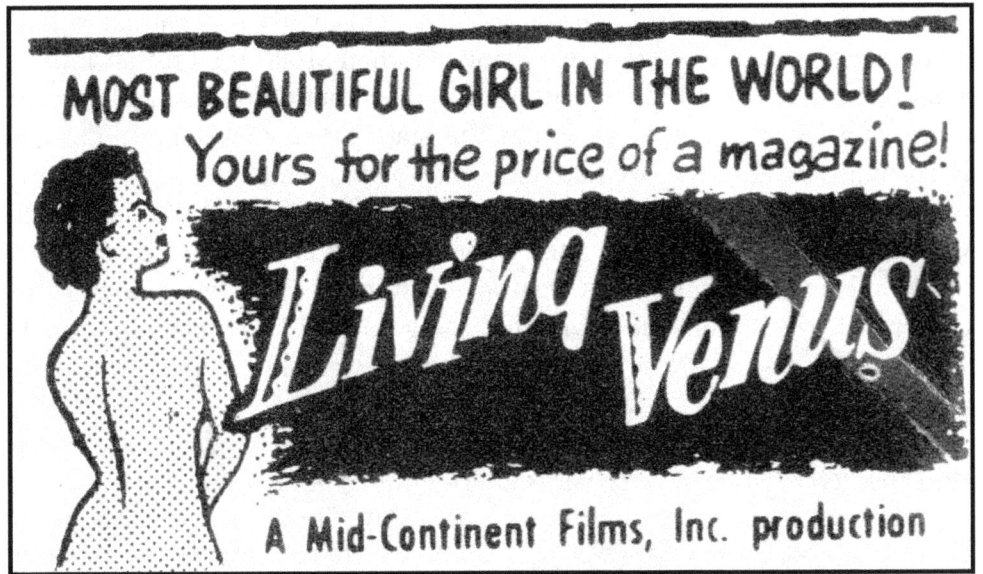

For one scene, we needed a swimming pool. Where were we going to find a swimming pool? We found a man in Lake Forest who had a genuine estate. We filmed the entire party sequence at his estate, and we used his swimming pool, and we shot almost an entire Friday night, which was to my consternation; we had an I.A. crew on that film, and they get overtime after 5:30. The deal that we made with this man — a man of great means — was that he would let allow us to shoot on his estate if we would let him play the role of the chauffeur, driving his own car! We really came out like gangbusters on that deal.

With the first screening of *Living Venus*, my hope sprang to life. I felt here was a playable picture — a film that theaters would indeed show — but beyond that, here was also a film that audience members would go out and tell other people, "Here is a film that you should go out and take a look at" — especially under the terms we could have as a low-budget movie. What I mean by that is, theaters at that time often based their prices for a movie on what they were paying in film rentals. So between Dave Friedman and Erwin Joseph, *The Prime Time* and *Living Venus* both went into distribution.

I was exalted until one night, late in the night, I realized we weren't getting any film rentals. The movies were playing — they weren't playing like blockbusters — but there were always bookings for the few prints we had. They were constantly in use. I began to feel like the wedding guest in "The Rime of the Ancient Mariner" — a sadder and wiser man. As it turned out, Modern Film Distributors had gone bust. And they owed Mid-Continent Films film rental money for both *The Prime Time* and *Living Venus*.

I had been the biggest investor, but many of my friends had put a little bit of money in. They had invested in me. So when Modern Film Distributors went bankrupt, I found myself out of money and out of friends. I was sitting there, and I had a temporary job as the staff director at United Film and Recording Studio, where we had cut *Living Venus*. In fact, my office — and I wouldn't really call it an office — was a desk sitting directly in front of their viewing screen! So whenever they wanted to look at a film, I had to either duck or leave the room. This was obviously one of the low points of my career. I thought, what the devil am I going to do? I had small children, to whom I had also made promises, and here I was sitting there with bare income, trying to cover whatever expenses I had.

Herschell Gordon Lewis's and David Friedman's next collaboration would be a "nudie-cutie" about a goofy voyeur who connects a series of vignettes featuring women in various states of undress. The two men collaborated on a script of sorts, finishing it in a mere six hours. The thin plot told the story of a ridiculous man who imagines that everyone he sees is naked. Both Lewis and Friedman agreed that their voyeur character should be based upon an infamous character named Lucky Pierre who had appeared at the center of a number of popular raunchy jokes in the 1930s. Lewis then came up with the title *The Adventures of Lucky Pierre*, and the two men established a new company they called Lucky Pierre Enterprises.

The two men then cast Billy Falbo, a comedian they had worked with previously on *Living Venus*, to play the film's protagonist. Advertising for the film touted that it was shot in "Fleshtone Color," "Cutie Color," and "Skinamascope." The film is significant as it would be the first nudie-cutie shot in 35mm color.

I still had the 35mm Mitchell camera that I had when I started Lewis and Martin Films. I also had a primitive recorder called a Uher. The benefit of the Uher was that it would put sound in sync with the picture. So, technically, I could still shoot a movie. I also had lights, which were totally out of date. They worked through a transformer. I had four of them. I remember someone said to me, "Your camera ought to be in the Smithsonian Museum." And I said, "Where do you think I got it?" You see, at some point as a filmmaker, you really become both sardonic and benevolent.

One day, Dave Friedman showed up with a deal. I had no idea if this was a good deal or a bad deal, but with things being as bad as they were, any deal made sense. I was sitting there at my little desk at United Film and Recording, and Dave said to me, "Al Sack, an independent film distributor from Dallas, Texas, will give us $7,000 if we can deliver one reel of pretty girls cavorting in the sun with some sort of a musical soundtrack." So I'm looking at this proposition: this man was going to give us $7,000 for one reel, which is a thousand feet of 35mm film. That runs about 90 feet a minute, so it was going to be about an 11-minute film. I had the lights and camera, and United Film and Recording had both a piano and an organ.

I said, "Here's what we can do for this $7,000. We'll buy ourselves a thousand feet of film, and we can buy another 400 feet for the slates. We can use my camera and record a soundtrack to go with it." Dave said he could get girls for about $50 each per day. I figured, well, we'd have four girls and have each one of them for a day. So after we added up all of our expenses, we figured we would end up with approximately $2,500 left over for each of us. And at that time, that was a small fortune. With the demise of Modern Film Distributors, Dave didn't have a job at all. And I really, in a sense, didn't have a job either. So what was to be lost by doing this?

In ancient Greek drama, they had a device called *deus ex machina*, which meant "god from machine." When Sophocles or one of those guys would write themselves into a corner, the solution was that a basket would come down from up above with a god in it. The god would then wave his arms and solve all of the problems. My *deus ex machina* in this instance turned out to be a sales representative named Jack Curtin, who worked for a laboratory in New York. I had already worked with Jack, as his company had handled the lab work on one of the previous films. Jack Curtin was really a kind of roving salesman, and he dropped in on me one day. He said, "What are you working on?" So I told him about our deal with Al Sack to make a one-reeler. Jack smelled blood and said, "Hold it right there. I'm gonna make you guys a deal. If instead of a one-reel film you will make a feature-length film of at least 70 minutes, no laboratory bills will be due until 90 days after we deliver the answer print to you." I was stunned by the confidence this fellow had based on my history in this business, although he, like everybody else, knew exactly what had happened there; the films I made had achieved distribution, they just hadn't gotten any money. Neither Dave Friedman nor I could see anything wrong with Jack Curtin's proposition. After all, it would be a lot easier for us to book a full feature-length film, and at that time, to be considered a feature-length movie that would play in a drive-in, a movie had to be at least 70 minutes long.

We then told Al Sack that we would not take his deal, but that we would give him distribution rights in Dallas of a movie we would make. What would that movie be? I was living in a town called Highland Park, Illinois, at that time, and Dave was living on Marine Drive in Chicago. We had become quite friendly through mutual misfortune. He came out to my house one weekend, and in a matter of hours, we wrote a bare-bones script we called *The Adventures of Lucky Pierre*. It was really the story of a knock-down comedian. But who would play the comedian? Well, again the forces of circumstance dictated this. In *Living Venus*, there's a scene where the character of the magazine owner has a party for his friends. And at that party, there's a comedian who entertains the guests. For that role, we had found a local nightclub comedian named Billy Falbo. He'd had just the goofy look and kind of cooperative spirit that we'd been looking for. So we then worked with Billy Falbo for a second time, and he became Lucky Pierre.

We shot *The Adventures of Lucky Pierre* in four days. It was October, and in Chicago, October can be hot, or October can be cold. Well, we weren't lucky — it was cold. But that made no difference, because we were going to shoot this thing one way or the other. We shot the film in and around a drive-in theater owned by a man Dave Friedman knew. That was one benefit that Dave Friedman always brought to the mix — he knew everybody in the movie business, or everybody knew him, which could be even more valuable. I never had to worry about contacts or who was going to do what. I had contacts in the production end, and Dave had contacts in the distribution end.

We bought ourselves 8,000 feet of 35mm color film, because one of Jack Curtin's deals — on behalf of the laboratory — was that the film had to be in color. Okay, so *The Adventures of Lucky Pierre* would be in color. Now we only bought 8,000 feet of film, and the film runs 6,300 feet. So once we cut the slates off, there really was nothing left.

We made *The Adventures of Lucky Pierre* with the same attitude with which we would have made Al Sack's one-reeler. I was the director and cameraman. Dave Friedman was the producer and soundman. And that was it. We were the entire crew. There were two scenes in the film that were sync takes — scenes in which people talk. The rest of the scenes just had background music. In those takes, because we had no crew, the actors had to work their own clapsticks, throw them aside, and then start acting. The imperative to them was, "Do it fast — we're running film!" There were two words that you would never hear on the set of *Lucky Pierre*: "Take two." I remember instructing a girl to stretch, and she misunderstood what I said. She thought I said, "Scratch." So she scratched herself. We left it in. It really made no difference for a movie like that.

There was nothing to cutting that movie. It was just a matter of assembling it. We simply cut the slates off and sent it to the laboratory. I got lucky again with the music for *The Adventures of Lucky Pierre*. I didn't have to write the music. There was a staff musician at United Film and Recording named Larry Wellington, who was sort of a quiet little genius at composing and recording themes, and he wrote the theme song to *Lucky Pierre*. And the only money we spent on the music aside from paying Larry, which was practically nothing, was what we paid to hire a flutist. Larry had suggested that this was the kind of background music we should have for the film, and we all agreed. Then there was the matter of mixing the sound-track.  Well, I think we mixed the picture as fast as it could run through the machine. Technically, there was no challenge at all. And that was fine. That wasn't the nature of this particular film.

We looked at *Lucky Pierre* as we were cutting it and said, "What have we done here? Who will ever play this picture?" We expressed that kind of remorse that you usually have in between making something and then determining whether it's going to be a success or failure. We then received the answer print from Jack's laboratory, and to be generous, it was ghastly.

This was in the days before computerized timing of movies, where a computer tells you whether to lighten or darken a scene. The lighting was all over the place. In my opinion — both then and now — it was totally unprofessional. "What are we going to do?" We had the answer print, and they would not give us more prints until we paid them money. We had 90 days to do that. We didn't know what we were going to do. All we had was this answer print, which would not have looked good on a Moviola, let alone in a theater.

Well, Dave Friedman had a friend named Tom Dowd, who later figured into a lot of the movies I made. Tom Dowd was a sweetheart who realized very quickly that there was a lot of money to be made in movies if you made the right kinds of movies with the right kind of distribution. At that time, Tom owned a little theater on the south end of Chicago's loop. It was on Wabash and Van Buren. The theater was called the Capri, and it played oddball pictures. And somehow, Dave convinced Tom Dowd to play *The Adventures of Lucky Pierre* at the Capri. But all we had was the answer print. I asked Jack Curtin if we could get a better quality print. He said, "Certainly — when you pay for the answer print." So we kind of scratched our heads and wondered what we were going to do. Well, Tom Dowd, not knowing the difference between an answer print and a release print, opened *Lucky Pierre* at the Capri, showing the answer print. It ran for nine weeks, and it broke the house record! Somehow, we were back in business with a vengeance. That it was such a horrible-looking movie seemed to make no difference at all. It was early enough in the cycle of that kind of movie that the people who came to see it didn't care. At that time, Russ Meyer was the only person making movies of this type that would be considered theatrically playable. The difference was that Russ' pictures were deadly serious and often in black-and-white. *Lucky Pierre* was a good-natured film, which covered a lot of mistakes. It wasn't intended to be artistic the way Russ Meyer's films were. It was intended to be funny, so people accepted the nature of the movie on every level. There's a good lesson to filmmakers: it's a lot better to appeal to the audience than to the critics.

When we saw the business *Lucky Pierre* was doing, it was completely startling. We were amazed that this film, which was as handmade as anything had ever been, could do this type of business. In its entire lifetime, *Lucky Pierre* only enjoyed a total of eleven prints. I am told that one of them still exists. A few years ago, Jimmy Maslon, who now owns most of my old movies, sent me a videocassette of the film. It was like having a child come home after having been away for a long time. I don't remember if I ever looked at it again, but I know that it still exists somewhere.

So that's the story of *Lucky Pierre*, and that truly put me back in the movie business at a time when I hadn't expected it to happen.

A postscript on *The Adventures of Lucky Pierre* . . . As I said, there were only eleven prints of the film ever in existence, and we literally played them to death. Well, one day a fellow named Eddie Ross, who owned a theater on Armitage Avenue in Chicago, called me in a semi-panic. It was a Wednesday, and he said, "You know we open our movies on Wednesday . . ." I said, "Yeah, so what?" And he said they had a miss-out, which meant the picture that was supposed to come in had never shown up. He asked, "What do you have that I can show until my movie shows up here?" I said, "The only thing we have is a print of *Lucky Pierre* that came in as a junk print to be destroyed." One of the things you learn in the movie business is that you never let somebody else tear up a print of your movie. You do it yourself. Otherwise, people end up bootlegging it. It's that kind of business. So this junk print was sitting on the floor in my office. I said, "That's all I have." And he said, "Send it over in a taxi right now. I need it. I've got to have something to show." This was around 10:30 in the morning, and they opened around eleven. So he was truly in a frenzy. He later called me around 1:30 in the afternoon. He said, "I want to thank you for sending me that print of *The Adventures of Lucky Pierre*. It broke my house record." I said, "In what way?" He said it fell apart six times, and his projectionist was busier trying to splice it back together than to show it. I said, "Did anybody walk out?" And he said, "Not in my theater." And that was how *Lucky Pierre* wrapped up its illustrious theatrical career.

The one difference between Dave Friedman and me is that I always tried to keep information to myself. Dave liked to talk about it. And he spread all over the industry how little *Lucky Pierre* had cost to make and how big business it was doing. And that did us a disservice to some extent because everybody else said, 'Hey, if these schmucks can do it, so can I!' " We literally spawned a lot of competition for ourselves just because of the success we had with *The Adventures of Lucky Pierre*.

We later discussed making a sequel to *The Adventures of Lucky Pierre*, but ultimately went in a different direction. Making a sequel made sense considering how much money we had made from the first film, and we even went so far as to discuss it with Billy Falbo. We had a sight gag figured out for the film. They would say, "Do you want your palm read?" And then they would paint the guy's hand with red paint. But, of course, that film was never made.

Daughter of the Sun - Nature's Playmates - Goldilocks and the Three Bares

"There is an old wives' tale that says where there is a nudist colony, there are beautiful naked young bodies. Not so. Unfortunately, quite the opposite is true."
— Herschell Gordon Lewis

After making a healthy profit from *The Adventures of Lucky Pierre*, Herschell Gordon Lewis and David Friedman set forth to make a fourth feature together. At the time, nudist colony films were making a lot of money. Little more than an excuse to show naked women frolicking in the sun, these films were made under the guise of being documentaries and were heavy on narration. Seeing the genre's potential for making money, Lewis and Friedman decided to make such a film. This time they had a substantially bigger budget with which to make the film, and Lewis immediately went to work on a treatment for the film. He quickly hammered out a twenty-five page outline, with Friedman contributing another six pages of dialogue. Because there were no nudist colonies anywhere near their home base of Chicago, the filmmaking duo located a suitable filming location in Miami, Florida. To separate their film from the other nudist colony pictures being made, Lewis and Friedman cast a stunning leading lady named Rusty Allen. *Daughter of the Sun* is notable as it would be the first of many Herschell Gordon Lewis films to feature actor Jerome Green (also known as Jerry Eden and Jerry Stallion, among other pseudonyms). It might also be noted that Lewis came up with the brilliant idea of filming the entire movie in black-and-white except for the nude scenes, which he filmed in color.

The film would ultimately be a huge success and would play for a number of years after its release.

The idea of making *Daughter of the Sun* came up because Dave Friedman, through his contacts, made it clear that if we produced such a picture, there were a number of theaters who automatically would play it (just as the majority of theaters automatically wouldn't play it). So both budget and speed became a factor, along with our desire to maintain a presence within the motion picture world. The bulk of the theaters who said they would play a picture of this type were the same ones that we were later able to negotiate with when we came up with *Blood Feast*, which broke new ground in every way you could use either of the words "broke" or "ground."

So, we came down to Florida to shoot this picture. We had made two decisions regarding this film: 1) that it would be a nudist camp picture, and 2) that anything that took place outside that area — the actual plotline, and I'm using a euphemism there — would be shot in black-and-white, because that wasn't why people were going to see these movies. But the camp scenes would all be shot in color. At that time, color film cost substantially more than black-and-white, and that's no longer true. Today, black-and-white is somewhat of a premium because everything has gone to color.

But who would we get to star in this film? Dave found a girl named Rusty Allen who was working as a waitress at some restaurant in Miami. She was remarkable — an absolute beauty. And she agreed, without any coaxing, to take the role in this film. This meant two things: 1) that there wouldn't be any embarrassment, which at that time there was, and 2) she had no background in acting whatsoever, so she wouldn't be very good in it. But the saving grace is that in a movie of this type, acting talent is of absolutely no consequence. In fact, that statement could be said to be true for most of the movies I made, where startling effects were far more important than acting talent. I mean, we weren't performing Shakespeare.

We located a nature camp. The people there — both the owners and the residents — were delighted to have a film crew there. The only downside was that they asked that every member of the crew take off their clothes and work in the nude. This, I guess, was for parity. But we didn't do that. I certainly didn't. I told them I had camera filters and equipment I had to carry and that I needed pockets. So, as long as I needed pockets, we would simply have to make ourselves invisible to the people there. I guess they were used to that, as they didn't give us any argument on that score.

We then shot both the color and the black-and-white scenes, and the fellow who played the male lead was named Jerome Green. He called himself Jerry Eden on that picture, and he later used other names on subsequent films we made together. Jerry, it turned out, was something of a fixer. He was

able to get things we needed. He was wired into some sort of underground economy there in Florida, so we found great value in that. As was typically our case, we used almost every foot of film we had.

In cutting it, I made a deal with an old friend from Chicago named Bill Johnson, and he cut this film in a very peculiar way. The synced sound takes were primarily reaction shots rather than the people speaking. I was uneasy with that, because we were cutting the negative directly. It's not like it is today where the last thing you do is cut the negative. At that time, once the negative was cut, if you were going to go back to it, you had a jump frame no matter what you did. And I didn't want that. So, okay, we left that as it was. And we assembled each print that came in since part of it was in black-and-white and part of it was in color. And to add a little bit more of what we might call a contemporaneous aspect to it, we had a scene or two before the opening credits.

We billed Rusty Allen as "the most beautiful girl in the world." That was our advertising campaign for *Daughter of the Sun*. We then put this film into release, and it did well from the very first day.

The funniest thing about *Daughter of the Sun* is that our distributor in Charlotte, North Carolina, who was an absolute sweetheart and a dear friend and certainly a crucial distributor for any picture we ever made, sent back a print. We wanted all of the prints clustered with us. It wasn't particularly desirable to have cans of film all over the place, but what we had learned in the movie business is that when you have cans of film out there in the world, they're playing somewhere and you're not getting any film rentals from those screenings. This particular distributor had wanted the film so badly that we'd had the lab send it directly to him. Back came this print, and all the black-and-white was in one piece to start it. All of the color scenes were in one piece at the tail end, and the film now made no sense at all. I called him and I said, "Harry, didn't you notice that in doing this, that about eight minutes before the movie was over it said, 'The End'?" He said, "Well, you had all this stuff before the beginning credits, so I didn't think it would matter if there was stuff after the end credits."

As was expected, *Daughter of the Sun* was a huge hit. Its first screening alone at Tom Dowd's Capri Theater brought in $2,300, which, as David Friedman wrote in his memoir was "a not-too-shabby figure for a four-hundred seat house with a two-dollar admission ticket." The savvy Dowd would soon play a crucial role in the creation of Lewis and Friedman's next picture. The theater owner offered the filmmakers

$3,000 each, plus all expenses, for another nudist camp film. The only catch? This time Dowd insisted that the film be a drama with a more elaborate storyline. Behind closed doors the two filmmakers had a chuckle over this, but they also saw the profitability of taking him up on his offer. Lewis and Friedman then went to work on a two-page synopsis of the film, and Dowd was satisfied.

The film, which paired Jerome Green (here billed as Scott Osborne) with Allison Louise "Bunny" Downe (as Vickie Miles), was a huge success and made Dowd a significant amount of money. He then not only paid Lewis and Friedman the money he had promised them, but gave them a respectable bonus, as well.

We were always prepared to make a movie with anybody and everybody who wanted to make a movie. We were geared to shoot almost instantaneously. I had an ancient Volkswagen bus crammed with obsolete

equipment, ready to go at any moment wherever anybody wanted to go. All we needed to buy was raw stock — film — and we were ready and willing to shoot a film. And nobody could match our price. Where were they going to go? Twentieth-Century Fox? Who else had a 35mm sound camera with all the gimmicks and the lights and so on, regardless of how antiquated the equipment might be? And who else could cut the film in a matter of days, let alone weeks or months? We had a lock on that kind of business at that time. And Tom Dowd wanted us to make another one of these pictures for him.

I don't really remember much about *Nature's Playmates* at all as it was another one of the boilerplate movies we turned out. I do remember that it starred Vickie Miles, who was sort of the young queen of that kind of film. She had already worked with K. Gordon Murray, who was a low-budget film producer from Miami of our vintage. The film had a little more polish to it than *Daughter of the Sun* had, and Vickie Miles was a much better actress than the actresses we had worked with previously.

A scene from the nudist camp film *Nature's Playmates*.

I don't know how much money that film made, but Tom Dowd never made a film that lost money. Not ever. We later made some movies together out in California, which he would not have done if he weren't prospering. And there was no reason for him not to prosper as he had all the right connections, which was really all that mattered in that business. Here's one funny thing about Tom Dowd: later on in our dealings with one another, Tom became enamored with French names. On some of those later films you will find a lot of cast and crew listed with fake French names. Tom felt that it was more artistic.

I'm told that *Nature's Playmates* was lost for some time, and I'll tell you why that is. Tom Dowd died about 20 years ago. His widow, a very nice woman, called to tell me that he had died after having moved to Clearwater, Florida. The Capri Theater was long gone by this time. She told me that when he learned that he was in a terminal condition, he instructed his son, Kevin, to carry all of his movies to the city junkyard and dump them. And

she said Kevin did this. I said, "Aren't you aware that there might be some residual value here?" She said, "Yes, I am aware, but for me there is no residual value." I don't know how many prints Tom had of any of these movies, but I do know that he had the negatives, which he apparently had his son dump.

After the success of *Nature's Playmates*, Tom Dowd once again enlisted the Lewis-Friedman team to make another picture for him. Dowd envisioned this film, initially titled *Singing in the Sun*, as the first nudie musical. For this film, Tom Dowd insisted that the team cast Rex Marlow as the lead. Marlow was a local piano player and singer that Dowd had discovered playing in a bar during a night out with David Friedman. Friedman felt that Marlow was a horrendous singer, but Dowd loved him and insisted that he play the lead in what would come to be titled *Goldilocks and the Three Bares*. Dowd also insisted on the casting of former light heavyweight champion of the world Joey Maxim.

Dowd's idea of making a nudie musical turned out to be ingenious, but his ideas for casting would turn out to be another story entirely. Marlow would ultimately turn out to be a double threat in that he couldn't sing and he couldn't act. Making all of this even more interesting was the fact that he had only nine fingers. During filming, Marlow would clutch the microphone stand with his right hand, drawing attention to the missing finger. When Lewis asked him politely not to hold the microphone stand with his right hand, Marlow would insist that "all the big singers" do it this way. To this, Lewis explained, "Yes, but the big singers have all their digits." Joey Maxim would prove to be equally problematic as he couldn't remember a single line of dialogue.

Billed as "the *Ben-Hur* of all nature camp movies," *Goldilocks and the Three Bares* would once again prove to be a money-maker for Dowd, Lewis, and Friedman.

Tom Dowd wanted to make a nudist musical. And that film, *Goldilocks and the Three Bares*, was, for its type, a relatively big movie. Tom believed that a movie of this kind could appeal to a much larger audience, and in that respect, I think he was about 30 years ahead of his time.

Rex Marlow, a Chicago nightclub singer and Tom Dowd discovery, was cast as the lead. He was an interesting character. Larry Wellington, who was the little musical genius who had composed the music for *The Adventures of Lucky Pierre*, joked, "Rex Marlow is starting a trend. He's bringing back off-key singing." Rex Marlow was not very popular on the set, as I remember. He felt that, rather than appearing in *Goldilocks and the Three Bares*, he should be appearing in a major Hollywood production in which Johnny Mercer would write the music and Shostakovich would write the score.

We also cast Joey Maxim in the film. This, like the casting of Rex Marlow, was something that Tom Dowd insisted upon. Joey Maxim was the former light heavyweight champion of the world, and Tom Dowd felt that Joey Maxim was a celebrity. Well, he may have been a celebrity, but an actor he was not. The problem with Joey Maxim is that he couldn't remember any of his lines, so we had to write them in the palm of his hand. So if you see that movie, you will see Joey Maxim constantly looking at the palm of his hand, which doesn't make a lot of sense if you don't know why he's looking at his hand.

Of course no one could remember the lines to any of the songs, but that wasn't a problem because we used boards on that film. This was before the days of teleprompter, and the boards would generally be held next to the camera. We wouldn't have used a teleprompter even if they had been available at the time, because teleprompters cost money, whereas writing out the lyrics on a board cost nothing.

We finished the movie and everyone involved with it was pleased. Well, I don't know if Rex Marlow was pleased, but everyone else was. Here was a movie that was exactly what had been promised and was turned in on-time and on-budget. Whether or not the notion of a nudie musical made any sense at all was not my decision to make. I showed up, handled the camera, told the actors, "Stand over there," and got out. Because it wasn't my film, I immediately lost touch with it, and really lost interest in it once we finished cutting it.

Boin-n-g! – Scum of the Earth – Bell, Bare and Beautiful

"Boin-n-g! came at a time when Dave and I felt that this marketplace was getting very crowded. It represented pretty much the same thing The Gore Gore Girls represented deep in the gore cycle — sort of a hail and farewell."

— Herschell Gordon Lewis

Herschell Gordon Lewis and David Friedman's next film, *Boin-n-g!*, would be their first of five collaborations with a man named Stan Kohlberg. Like Tom Dowd, Kohlberg was a theater owner (he owned a handful of drive-in theaters and three hardtops). And like Dowd, Kohlberg wanted to make some money in the filmmaking business. He had never screened nudies at his theaters, but he recognized their potential for making money.

This film, which would feature much more slapstick than the filmmaking duo's previous efforts, would tell the story of two would-be filmmakers who set out to make their own nudie film. In telling this story, Lewis and Friedman were able to poke fun at the filmmakers and distributors of such films, and also to comment on the general lack of quality associated with them. At the end of *Boin-n-g!*, the inept filmmakers (played by Bill Kerwin and Bill Johnson) screen their film for a local theater owner. After watching the film, the theater owner proclaims that it is the worst film he has ever seen and then adds, "I'll take it!"

We shot that film at an estate in a northwest area outside of Chicago. I was handling the advertising for a client called The Robert Bartlett Realty Company. The son of Robert Bartlett, Dick Bartlett, was very much interested in making movies. He arranged for us to shoot this movie on their estate out in the woods about forty miles outside of Chicago. And that was a break for us.

This was our first film working with distributor Stan Kohlberg, and we even shot a scene in one of his theaters. At that time, all of the parties — Dave, myself, Stan, and his partner, Sid Reich — were very enthusiastic about the partnership. That the enthusiasm waned later on, in my opinion, was strictly due to Stan Kohlberg's greed. I don't think he could stand the thought of anyone else making money, even if the deal had been set up that way beforehand. Later on, the three of us wound up in court suing him over *Two Thousand Maniacs*, and the collaborative partnership then split apart.

The stars, and I use that word advisedly, were the old standbys like Bill Kerwin. By that time, Bill Kerwin had decided more than I had that he was going to be available anytime I shot anything. I think one reason for this was that there was never any pressure on our set. When Bill was shooting commercials, which were the only other kind of work an actor in Chicago could have, it was always, "quick, quick" and "you didn't do this right." There was never any of that on our sets. It was always a very happy time, and I think he recognized that. The other actor was Bill Johnson, who was more of a producer than anything else (although he later played the doctor in *The Pill*). Bill owned even more obsolete moviemaking equipment than I did, and that made him quite valuable to us. If we couldn't get a zoom lens working, we'd just borrow one from Bill Johnson. He also looked like the standard all-American boy; not handsome, and not athletic, but average. He was absolutely the average guy, which made him perfect for this role. The third actor's name was Robbie Bee, and he played Schmurtz, the photographer.

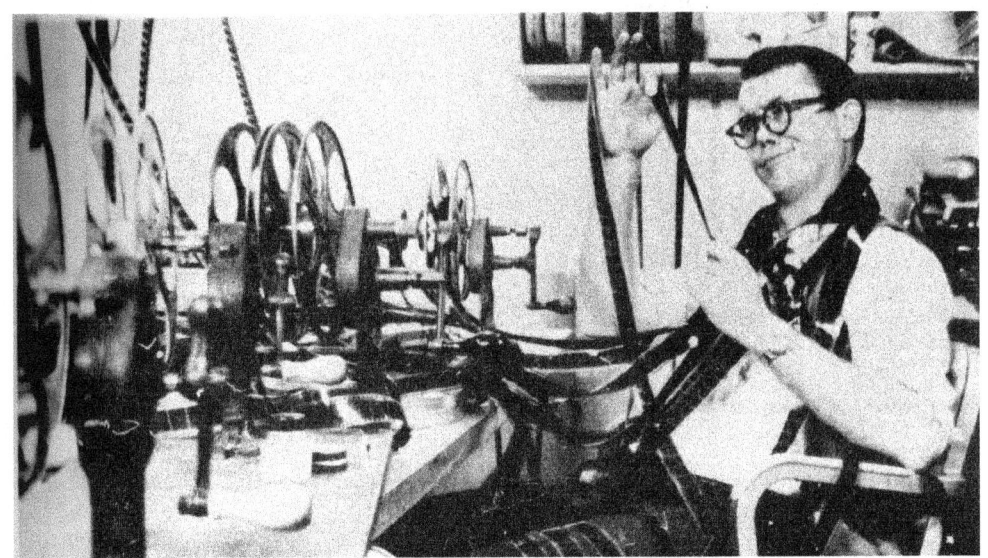

Larry Aberman in a scene from Herschell Gordon Lewis's film *Boin-n-g!*.

Actress Vickie Miles came back again for this movie. Vickie's birth name was Louise Povoromo, which she'd changed to Allison Louise Downe. She had then appeared in a couple of K. Gordon Murray's movies under the name Bunny Downe. Vickie Miles then wound up appearing in our films after K. Gordon Murray mentioned her to Dave. Eventually it became apparent to me that she had other value beyond just her acting. The value she had was that she knew everyone in the business in Miami, which we did not. If we wanted to shoot in the Deauville Hotel, which was absolutely impossible, it would then become possible through some possibly subterranean connection she had.

There was another girl in this movie named Joanne Rotolo, whom I believe had been recruited by Vickie Miles. She then became the favorite of Dick Bartlett, which helped us. The other two girls were simply pretty girls that we used.

My old friend and former partner, Martin Schmidhofer, from Lewis and Martin Films, also appeared in *Boin-n-g!* He happened to be in town and wanted to come to the set. He said, "What can I do? How can I help?" We had him appear in the film as an Indian chief. We put a headpiece on him and gave him a hatchet. His character is told that there's no reason to look at these girls, but then when he sees them he says, "White man lie." Marty had his moment onscreen after all those years behind a camera.

For production we rented a gadget that was very much like a cherry-picker, although it wasn't as big, and it certainly wasn't as safe. I would be up at the top — I doubled as the cameraman on this project — and unless someone stood on the platform, it was very likely it would tip over. If no one had been standing there, it would have spilled me and my camera out onto the ground. And we didn't have a zoom lens. So, you will see some shots in *Boin-n-g!* in which the camera was dropped by simply cranking it down. That was an experiment in production that seemed to pay off all right. One benefit to a movie of this type is that nobody pays much attention to production.

In the film, these guys make a terrible movie in which everything goes wrong. Then they finally screen it for a distributor, who was played by my buddy Larry Aberman (appearing as Larry Aberwood). The distributor then says, "It was the worst movie I've ever seen! I'll take it!" People have asked me if *Boin-n-g!* was in any way autobiographical. I suppose you could say the story was autobiographical in that it was about two people guessing what the market was who had absolutely no background in the visual aspects of glamour and taking a shot. But that wasn't quite true, because by that time we had made a few pictures. We had some notion — just from sitting anonymously in audiences — of when people would get bored and turn their heads away or get up to go to the concession stand. So, it was more autobiographical about the way we started out than the way we were at the time we made that film.

Boin-n-g! was a title that I simply made up. What was funny was that, as we were cutting the film, a big studio film titled *Boeing Boeing* starring Tony Curtis was released to theaters. It was a comedy about airplane pilots, and we felt that if people confused the two pictures, then God bless us. I'd just as soon have that kind of confusion.

Boin-n-g! was not what I would call a major enterprise, but from the viewpoint of time and from the viewpoint of budget versus results, it had merit. This was the kind of film where making a mistake was almost impossible. And with that in mind, I would point out the following to anyone who might be reading this. If someone is considering making a motion picture, whether it's on film or digital, one of the primary questions to ask yourself going in is, "Do we have something that someone is going to enjoy?" That's a major factor. When I watch a film at home, about half the time I find myself saying, "Good God, who made this, and why?" And that's the end of it.

Boin-n-g! hit a high note of entertainment. There was nothing anybody could attack on that film. It didn't insult the audience. If anything, it insulted the characters in the film. If you can make a movie that has that effect — where the audience feels superior — you've got a winner, no matter what the budget might be.

None of the people involved with the film had any problem with the final product. *Boin-n-g!* did very, very well at the box office for a lengthy period of time. There wasn't really much about it in terms of plotline that made any sense, but that didn't seem to matter to anyone.

Herschell Gordon Lewis' next effort, *Scum of the Earth*, would be a departure from the nudie-cuties. This dark film would tell the story of pornographers seeking to exploit a young would-be model. The film again starred Vickie Miles and Bill Kerwin (as Thomas Sweetwood).

Despite its being a minor project made primarily as an excuse for Lewis and Friedman to return to the warmer climate of Miami, the film is significant because it is the last film Lewis made in black-and-white, and also because it was the first film made in the dark exploitation cycle known as the "roughies." (These were films that featured violence against women, such as kidnapping, rape, and murder.)

Scum of the Earth was the last movie I shot in black-and-white. We made that picture knowing it was the last film we'd ever make in black-and-white. The decision was made deliberately, because at that time, shooting in color didn't cost much more at all. But we wanted a sort of gritty effect for this picture, and I think we got it. We compensated for the lack of color by making everything else as contemporaneous as possible.

Vickie Miles played the ingénue in that film. Mal Arnold, who later played Fuad Ramses in *Blood Feast*, played a tough kid. That was where we met Mal Arnold. It struck me immediately that he was very cooperative on set, and this was a major factor for directors like me. I didn't want any dissension on the set. We just wanted to shoot and go on to the next scene, shoot and go on to the next scene. "Oh, it's eight o'clock? Too bad." Shoot and go on to the next scene. In that respect, Mal Arnold was our kind of guy. So later on when it came time to cast Fuad Ramses, whose age could have been anything, we remembered Mal.

Scum of the Earth was like any movie I ever made in that it didn't really matter who we cast. Who cared who was in it? Yeah, Harvey Korman was in *Living Venus*. So what? Henny Youngman was in *The Gore Gore Girls*. So what? Did people go to see those people? Recently I read an article about Robert De Niro having prostate cancer or something of that sort, and some rather cynical critic wrote, "Do people go to a movie because Robert De Niro is in it?" And that's true. You don't go to see a movie because Robert De Niro is in it. Or Henny Youngman. Or Karen Black, who made her debut in *The Prime Time*. We had Tim Holt in *This Stuff'll Kill Ya!* Tim Holt had been the young star of *The Treasure of the Sierra Madre*. But who knew or cared about Tim Holt? Could I have built an advertising campaign around Tim Holt? (Especially at the time when I got him, where he was in his absolute last period of decline.) I don't believe it makes any difference at all who is or isn't in a movie. Especially when a movie pitches itself as itself rather than something that has Johnny Depp in it. I see that Disney apparently offered Johnny Depp $75 million to appear in the next *Pirates of the Caribbean* movie. That baffles me. If I was a Disney stockholder, I would question that kind of offer. And the article I read said he's "evaluating" the offer, which I also think is funny. After all, all of the *Pirates of the Caribbean* movies are the exact same movie over and over again.

Our old friend Bill Kerwin, appearing here as Thomas Wood, played a photographer. While we were making this film I predicted (rather unpleasantly) that someday Bill was going to die of lung cancer. He would light up a cigarette at every possible opportunity. One rule I had that I imposed on

every single set I had was that there was no smoking on the set. But Bill, because he was part of our family, felt he could ignore that. Smoke hovers in the air. You may not think you're seeing it, but it gives a peculiar effect on camera. I didn't want that. I wanted clear images, but he was always smoking. On some occasions, we actually left the cigarette in the shots, which meant that we then had to match the length of the burning cigarette from shot to shot for continuity. But that was how Bill was, and I'm sad to report that he ultimately died of lung cancer.

The plotline of *Scum of the Earth* was a fairly grim one. They try to seduce this girl into a life of sin. The heavy in the film was played by Larry Aberman (appearing as Lawrence J. Aberwood). We tried a technique there which later became very popular with better known movies. As he began to grind out a threat, we would shoot a sentence or so, and then move in tighter. We didn't zoom. The scene was cut this way; we would cut tighter for the next sentence. And then cut tighter for the next sentence after that, until all you could see were his teeth. That's how tight we were. And he had a lot of bridgework, which I thought might spoil the effect. But subsequently I was told that that made it even more dramatic.

Scum of the Earth was shot entirely in black-and-white with the exception of a single frame. There had been a movie made some years before starring Jean Harlow called *Red Dust*. In that film, there was a scene in which one frame was tinted red. That had stuck with me all those years. So when we got to that scene where he sticks the gun in his mouth at the end of the film, he pulls the trigger and there was a single red frame. Film goes through a projector at twenty-four frames per second, and each frame is on the screen for one-fiftieth of a second. People outside of the industry would say, "Who could ever see that?" They see it. They say, "What was that red flash?" This is especially effective when there's someone onscreen with a gun in his mouth and is shooting. Audiences understand the nature of that red flash. Again I have sat in theaters and observed people watching this, and it does bring a reaction.

In the film, when the police are chasing Larry Aberman down the street near the 163th Street shopping mall in Miami, we had two real cops. Who else would you hire to wear a police uniform? This way you don't pay for the uniforms. They were chasing this guy down the street, and people not only stopped to stare, but on occasion a big burly man would show up and try to grab him to help the police. Then they supposedly chase him across the beach to this motel, which was the Suez Motel, where we always stayed on these shoots. They were chasing him in front of the Suez, and people were out on their balconies. We asked these people to step inside so we could shoot for three or four minutes, and some woman on the second floor yelled, "I'm paying $60 a day for this room, and you want me to go back inside? Not on your life!" So we had to shoot around that, which was funny. Such is the nature of independent filmmaking. Had it been Robert Redford, she probably would have gone back inside in exchange for an autograph. I don't think Larry Aberman's autograph would have gotten us very far.

Scum of the Earth ultimately became the first film in a cycle known as "the roughies." This happened because we were trying to avoid following the beaten path. I felt this was simply a good business practice, because others could eventually follow that path better than we had initially trod it. We could walk the path, but they could eventually pave it. We wanted to make a type of movie where people would come out of the theater talking about something other than the rotten acting (although I must say the acting really wasn't too bad in this film) or the low production value. Instead, people came out of the theater saying, "Boy, that was rough stuff!" So, I guess you could say *Scum of the Earth* has a distinguished history. It was the first of its kind, which was something I didn't really think about at the time. It was like *Blood Feast*; sure, I knew that no one had made a film like this before, but I never intended to start a trend. I simply wanted to make a movie that might find an audience to watch it.

Herschell Gordon Lewis and David Friedman were approached by two theater owners and would-be film producers named Eli Jackson and Leroy Griffith. Like Tom Dowd before them, Jackson and Griffith sought to hire the team to make a nudie-cutie. The catch? Eli Jackson wanted the film to star his wife, burlesque performer Virginia Bell. Neither Lewis nor Friedman was familiar with Virginia Bell, but a number of people assured them that she was well-known in the burlesque circuit. Lewis and Friedman agreed to make the film, which they would ultimately title *Bell, Bare and Beautiful.*

Because Lewis and Friedman were in agreement that Virginia Bell's face was somewhat less attractive than the voluptuous 48-24-36 figure she was best known for, they sought creative ways to shoot around her face. Making things more interesting, the filmmakers learned while shooting that Bell was pregnant. "[She was] three months pregnant," Lewis has been quoted as saying, "and I could only hope, while we were shooting the picture, that she wouldn't trip and fall on me."

Dave Friedman and I had now developed somewhat of a reputation in the nudie film business. I wasn't thrilled with it, because I had small children. At the time, I didn't really see the direction that kind of film was taking. Once I did, I figured it was time to get out of that racket and go out and make a different kind of film. But in that period in between came a film called *Bell, Bare & Beautiful*.

Bell, Bare & Beautiful featured a young woman named Virginia Bell. She was known in the burlesque world as Virginia "Ding-Dong" Bell, and her chief asset was her 48-inch bosoms. And this was before people were having surgeries to get big bosoms; she simply had a big bosom. Virginia Bell was well known in the burlesque arena because of her ability to walk around on stage with these huge protrusions in front. But that was the extent of her talent, in my opinion. She was married to a man who owned a theater in Cincinnati. His name was Eli Jackson. Eli and a fellow named Leroy Griffith, who owned a theater on Washington Street in Miami, became partners to make this movie.

Our old buddy, Bill Kerwin, played the male lead under the name Thomas Sweetwood. One of the actresses, and I'm using a euphemism here, was a woman named Joy Hodges. She was actually the mother of one of the other actresses in the film. She was about 60 years old and still stripping.

We shot the film in Miami at the same nature camp we had worked in before. This was another of our four-day productions. This was a case where this wasn't my movie; we were making it for someone else. As it turned out, Virginia Bell was pregnant. This was something we learned on the first day of shooting. Because of this, we either had to shoot that movie right then or never at all. So, we shot it right then, and we shot it in four days.

The film's plotline was primitive if existent at all. In that instance, we simply shot it, assembled it, and sent it off to these two fellows, who then put the movie into release. Like Tom Dowd, these fellows had an edge on us, and that was that they owned theaters that played these types of movies. This gave them the ability to say to other theater owners making these types of movies, "If you play our movie, we'll play yours." As a business proposition, that made a lot of sense. And I will say for Eli and Leroy, they paid the bill, there was never any question, and the movie got finished. And that was it. It was then out of my hands, as it was made on contract for someone else.

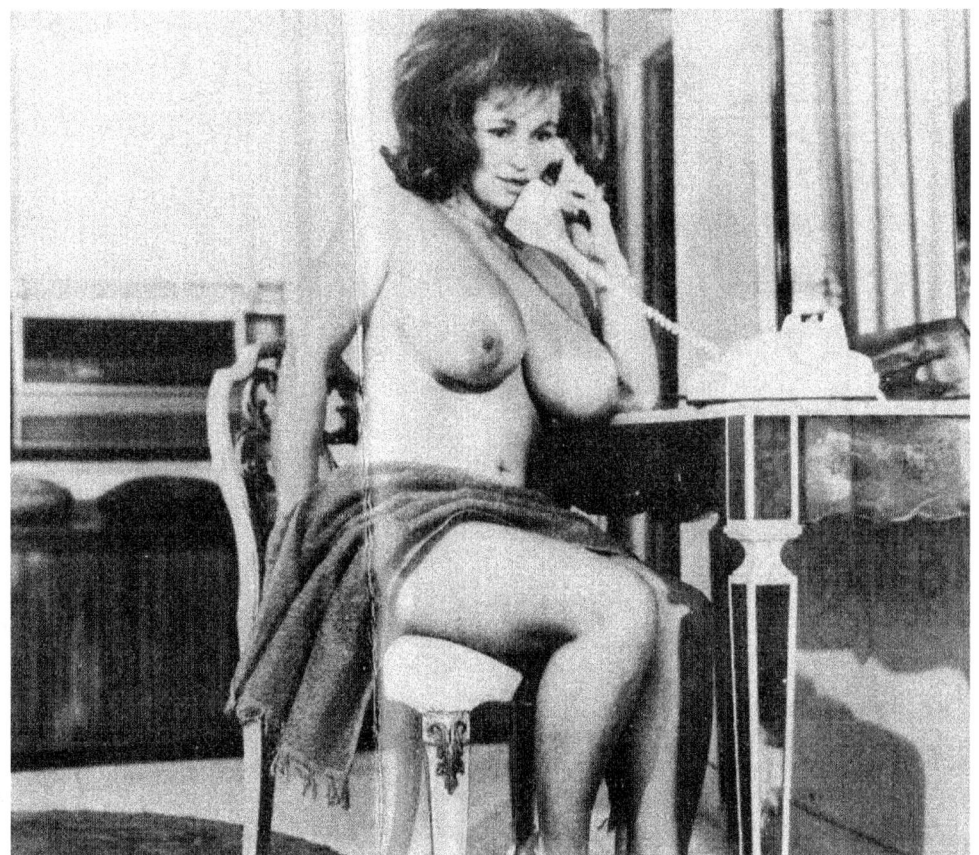

A scene from *Bell, Bare & Beautiful* featuring actress Virginia Bell.

One of the aspects of *Bell, Bare & Beautiful* was that it tied us to the next film, which was *Blood Feast*. And the decision to make that film was made so abruptly that many of the same actors and actresses would ultimately appear in both films. For example, a fellow named Al Gordon, who used the pseudonym "Al Golden" in *Bell, Bare & Beautiful*, played the part of a doctor. Then in *Blood Feast*, he became a lecturer on Egyptian history. Mal Arnold was a young tough in *Bell, Bare & Beautiful*, and he of course went on to play Fuad Ramses in *Blood Feast*. We shot those two pictures back-to-back, so they had some relationship with one another.

Blood Feast — Two Thousand Maniacs! — Color Me Blood Red

"I've often compared Blood Feast *to a Walt Whitman poem; it's no good but it's the first of its kind."*
—Herschell Gordon Lewis

Herschell Gordon Lewis' next film, *Blood Feast*, would prove to be a cinematic milestone and the film for which Lewis is most remembered for today. As Christopher Wayne Curry notes in his book A TASTE OF BLOOD: THE FILMS OF HERSCHELL GORDON LEWIS, *Blood Feast* was "intentionally plotless and near mindless." But plot would matter little in this new type of exploitation film Lewis was creating. Featuring dismembered limbs, gouged-out eyes, and buckets full of prop blood, *Blood Feast* would become the first gore film ever made.

The film's script would be credited to Allison Louise Downe, but was actually little more than a skeletal 14-page outline. (The film's actual shooting script would be assembled by the cast and crew as filming progressed.) The first actor Lewis cast in *Blood Feast* was Bill Kerwin,

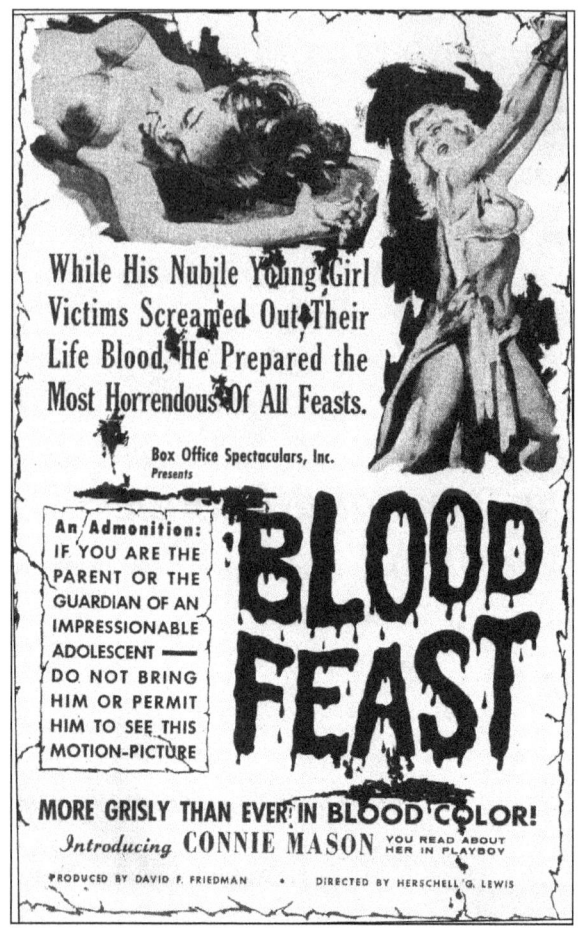

who shortened his Thomas Sweetwood moniker to Thomas Wood. Sandy Sinclair, who had appeared previously in *Scum of the Earth*, was the second performer cast. Lyn Boulton, Jerome Green, and Scott Hall were then cast shortly thereafter. Despite heavy opposition from Lewis, Friedman discovery and *Playboy* Playmate Connie Mason was soon added to the film's cast. "She never knew a line," Lewis has been quoted as saying. "Not ever." For her troubles Miss Mason received $175. Mal Arnold would ultimately be cast in the film's most pivotal role as the villain, Fuad Ramses.

The film's budget would be rather small at $24,500, and the entire shoot would last only nine days. Despite this, *Blood Feast* would be one of the most influential films ever produced. Its impact can be seen not only in the gore films that followed in its bloody wake, but also in violent mainstream films such as *The Wild Bunch* and *Reservoir Dogs*. As Lewis himself is quick to point out, *Blood Feast* isn't all that great a film in terms of quality, but it would forever change the cinematic landscape.

The history of *Blood Feast* is certainly no secret to anyone in the business. I don't know that there's ever been a movie of this type, or lack of budget, that's had so much notoriety. I wanted to risk making the kind of film that nobody else was making, but I didn't want to spend any money doing it because it was entirely possible that nobody would ever show this movie, or if someone did, nobody would ever go to watch it. And the result of all this was *Blood Feast*.

We had no script. We gave Allison Louise Downe screenplay credit for the film, but in reality the script came together piece by piece as we shot the film. I believe the final "script" we wound up with only resulted in about 14 pages, and it had only really been assembled for cutting purposes, which was really superfluous anyway, as there weren't enough outs to cut out of there. We used absolutely every bit of footage that wasn't completely terrible in putting that picture together.

We were cutting this film in my little cutting room in Chicago, and people would wander by and see this horrible-looking thing with grease pencil marks all over it. They would ask, "Did you shoot a medical film?" No one could understand what this film was all about. As you can imagine, this did not add to my peace of mind about the project. I thought, Oh, my God, what have we done here? Then, when I was getting estimates for a musical score for the picture, I came close — really, really close — to scrapping the entire score altogether and leaving the whole thing to Johann Strauss and John Philip Sousa. The problem I had was that I knew what I wanted. I could almost hear the entire score played out in my head at night. And when I was getting estimates to score that picture — and these were from el cheapo sources — it was more money than the entire picture cost to make. Here I was faced with a decision.

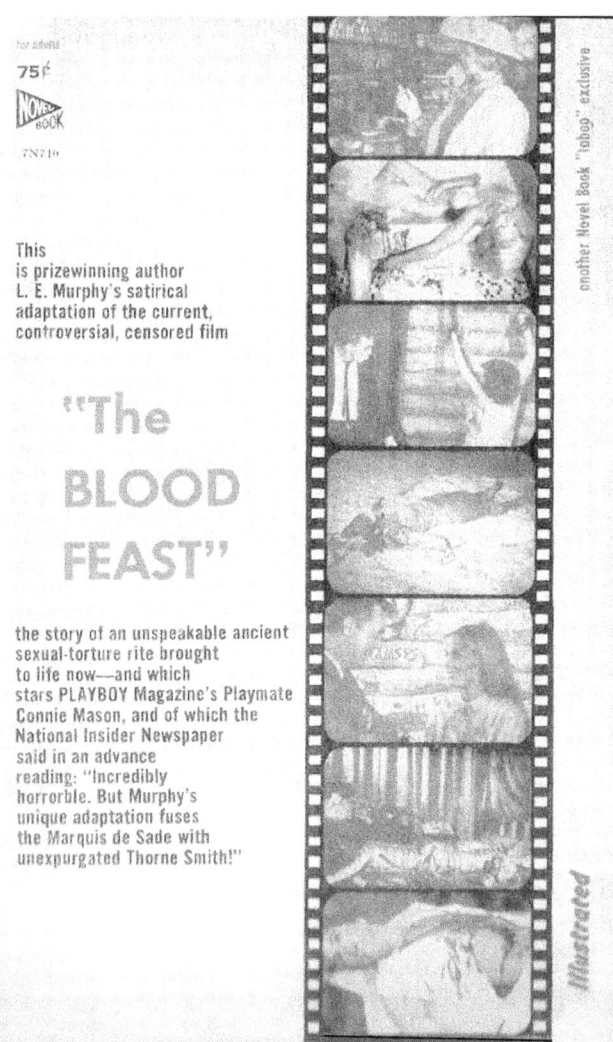

The cover of the paperback novelization of Lewis's *Blood Feast*.

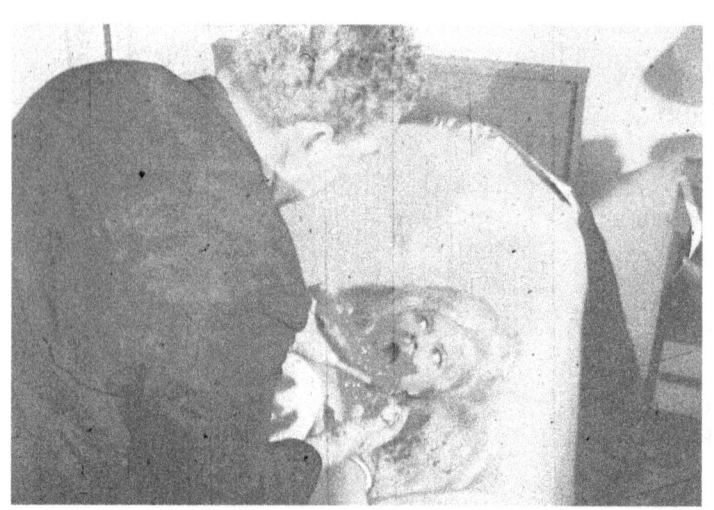

The infamous tongue scene featuring Astrid Olsen from the film *Blood Feast*.

As a kid, like everyone else, I took violin lessons, so I had some minor background in music (albeit not enough to orchestrate a score). But it became that kind of challenge, where all I could do was score the film myself or use prerecorded music, which wasn't all that cheap either. Or, I could have sat down at an organ and just put together some transitional chords, but I felt that would damage whatever impact we might have had in that movie. So I bit the bullet, and I scored that picture myself, and I have never worked so hard in all my life! But I can tell you as a veteran of many movies and many books on marketing, of all the feelings of accomplishment that I have had, I don't know of any that matched recording the music of *Blood Feast* and having it sound the way it sounded in my head. I was ready to go out and write a symphony after that! Of course I didn't do that, but I did do much of the music for *Two Thousand Maniacs!*.

The Suez Motel ultimately became the basis of *Blood Feast*. Outside the Suez was a small eight-foot-tall sphinx, and that gave us the notion for the Egyptian overtones. I then just selected the most Egyptian name I could think of — Fuad Ramses. And you know, that name, Fuad Ramses, has remained popular up until today. Online there are people who use the name as their handle, and there is even a FuadRamses.com, which I think is funny. I don't have anything to do with that, but I do think it's something of a tribute.

We shot *Blood Feast* in just a few days with a cast of nobodies. Dave Friedman cast *Playboy* playmate Connie Mason at the Playboy Club in Miami, where he also enlisted Astrid Olsen. As you now know, Astrid Olsen has also become an icon in horror film history because of the size of her mouth. We needed someone who could fit a second tongue inside her mouth for the infamous gore scene. Try that sometime and you will find that it's not only not easy to have a second tongue in your mouth, but it's actually impossible to breathe! But it was not impossible for Astrid Olsen.

The famous tongue scene, which has really become the watershed scene for all splatter movies — to this day, that scene is often called the beginning of the splatter film — begins with a shot of a drunk (played by Dave Friedman) driving up with Astrid Olsen in a convertible. He then takes her to the door and leaves her. Meanwhile, our cello was playing (deliberately, I might add) an off-key version of an old drinking song called "How Dry I Am." So Astrid goes inside and the drunk disappears. At that point, there's a rather ominous knock on her door. She opens up the door and lets out one scream. This was all filmed at the Suez Motel. We had tipped everyone off that we were going to shoot this thing, but apparently the word didn't filter all the way down. But it made no difference; she was going to scream, we were going to get her inside that room, and then people could just wonder what was happening. The script calls for Fuad to push her down to the bed, and then, while she's gurgling away, he reaches into her mouth and pulls out her tongue.

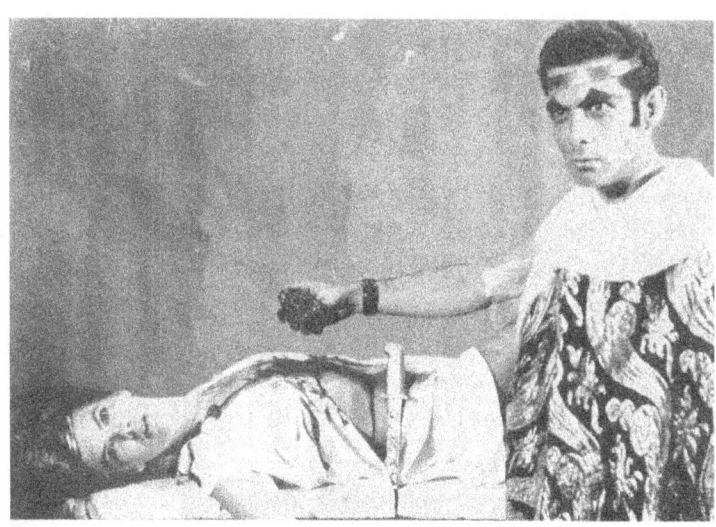

Fuad Ramses (Mal Arnold) lays waste to *Playboy* Playmate Connie Mason in this scene from *Blood Feast*.

We had great difficulty locating a tongue. The only tongue we could find from any source, whether it was the supermarket or a butcher shop, was the piece they cut off to sell you in the store. We needed the entire tongue, which has a lot of crap hanging behind it. In order to get a tongue of that complexity, we had to send off to a packing house in Tampa. That tongue was our one touch of luxury on that film. Somehow we were clairvoyant in that we knew this scene would have people talking in a way that no scene in such an inexpensive picture ever had. So we got the tongue and kept it inside this little refrigerator in our room at the Suez, and then paid no attention to it. I don't know if the refrigerator wasn't properly plugged in or what, but there was a heat wave, and you could smell that tongue two blocks away. Now what? We couldn't send to Tampa for another tongue, because we had to shoot that scene later that same day. So before we used the tongue in the scene, we doused it heavily with stage blood, which was Kaopectate-based, and gelatin, and that worked an absolute miracle. When she flops over and that stuff comes out of her mouth, it is truly a nauseating scene, which was absolutely what we wanted it to be. That scene worked, and I think the proof that it worked is that even today people tend to compare their shots with the tongue scene from *Blood Feast*.

Connie Mason was never an actress on the level of a Reese Witherspoon, but she regarded herself on that level, and she felt that she was a personal friend of Hugh Hefner's. All of this gave her a posture that was something less than positive. She could not remember any of her lines, and the hotel wanted to throw us all out because of the condition of her room — lipstick on the mirrors, and whatever else she had done. But she was there.

We shot the brain-snatching sequence outside on a beach shared by the Suez Motel and another motel called The Colonial. We actually shot that on a moonlit Saturday night, with the blessing of the Suez management. Dave always wanted to put a snake in a picture, so okay, we had a snake. It made no sense at all under any circumstances, and it cost us an extra $50 to rent, but it was for Dave, so we put the snake in the picture. Well, the doggone

thing got loose on the beach. Scott Hall, an old Ringling Bros. veteran who had become an actor, grabbed a cardboard box and ran and captured the snake inside the box. The purpose of the shot was for a couple to be making love on the beachfront, and Ramses sneaks up, conks the guy over the head, and then snatches the brains from where brains would be if this hadn't been an actress. People were standing out on their balconies watching this. They knew it was a movie, because we had our big Mitchell camera there. It wasn't like we were trying to make it look like someone was really smashing in somebody's head out there. But because there had never been a film like this before — certainly not for the kind of demographic that populated the Suez or the Colonial — it was rather startling to people. And those folks didn't move at all. I even shouted out to them through a megaphone and instructed them not to talk until they heard one of us yell, "Cut!" And whenever we would yell "cut," you could immediately hear the burbling come back all at once.

While we were shooting that scene, my cameraman, Roy Collodi, was loading a magazine for the Mitchell. I looked down at the changing bag and I saw that it had not been zipped shut. Roy said he didn't know it was supposed to be zipped shut, and I said, "That's what the zipper's there for." I didn't know what to do, because we had already gone through one roll of film. So we took a chance, and we were lucky — the roll had not been light-struck. If it had been, I don't know what we would have done. There was, it appears, an angel resting on our shoulder for that shot.

The place we used as Fuad Ramses' headquarters was a pizza parlor, and it was right on a main street. We needed an arm that would be found baked. To give it the right appearance, we took it out in the street and doused it with gasoline. Well, the gasoline caught fire, and we couldn't put it out. When we eventually got it out, it had burned a huge round hole in the asphalt. We tried to melt some asphalt to run into the hole so no one would break an axle, but we weren't overly successful in this endeavor. Fortunately for us, there were no police officers around, so we grabbed the smoldering appendage and got the heck out of there. I'm sure they wondered for months what happened in that street.

I notice that sometimes people will criticize the lack of sophistication to the plot of *Blood Feast*. Well, to this day I reject that argument on the grounds that a sophisticated plotline would have been very much at odds with the primitive nature of the way we shot it. We paid very little attention to anything that might have added production value if it did nothing to add to the shock value. I've read critiques where they complain that we didn't move our camera much, and to this I say so what? That had nothing whatever to do with what we were doing there. That's not why people go to a movie; they

A grisly scene from Herschell Gordon Lewis's film *Blood Feast*.

go to a movie so they can walk out saying one of three things: 1) "That was funny," 2) "I was entertained," or 3) in the case of *Blood Feast*, "Holy smoke, did you see that?" And enough people had that third reaction that it set the ground for us to make *Two Thousand Maniacs!* and then continue making that kind of motion picture for several years. And we had no competition, because others were afraid to come into our little parlor.

    The advertising campaign for *Blood Feast* also broke new ground. We had barf bags made to be given out in the theaters. No one had ever had a barf bag before. On the barf bag it said, "You may need this when you see *Blood Feast*." In some cases where we played in a hardtop theater, we had an ambulance parked outside with its lights going. We had nurses in the lobbies in case someone passed out, threw up, or had a heart attack. We used gimmicks that had never been done before, and are now quite common today. Dave Friedman even went so far as to apply for — and receive — an injunction so that the film could not play in Sarasota, Florida. This got us a lot of press, and no one knew that the man who got the injunction against the film was actually its producer. This was easy to do as Sarasota had some sort of internal regulation against movies of this type, so we just asked them to go ahead and implement that regulation. Dave was absolutely the consummate showman — if there was anything to be exploited, he would undoubtedly find a way in which to exploit it. The campaign, which we worked on jointly, was an absolute smash.

Theaters that we believed would never take a chance on a picture of this sort took a chance. Many wouldn't. To this day there are theaters who won't play a picture of that sort — not because the films are cheap and schlocky, but because the theaters don't believe the classic moviegoer will respond to a movie like that. And if you look at *Blood Feast*, there's no nudity. There are no "F" words, which have now become common even in comedies that are PG-13. So I have no apologies to make for that picture under any circumstances.

Our movie was banned in England for many years. In the early 1990s, I was invited to a screening in London at a theater in Soho. When I showed up at the theater, I found that it had changed itself for the day into a private club. That was the out in England — if it showed in a private club, then it was all right. But if you showed it in a general theater, you would find yourself in hot water because that was illegal. So this theater simply changed itself into a private club, and the place was absolutely packed, wall-to-wall. And those people had to join the club for that day in order to see this movie.

And this was not unusual for us. We were actually the progenitors of legislation in a number of places where there had never been any prohibition of movies of this type — largely because there had never been any movies of this type. I remember screening this personally (because we had no one else to send) for the Kansas Censor Board, which was a group of older women in Kansas City, Kansas. I screened this movie, and on came the titles. One of these women said, "Oh, you were the composer?" And I said, "Yes, I am." And that was the last civil conversation throughout the screening. Another horrible thing there: they screened this film at almost double the speed. Apparently they had a lot of films to screen, and they simply didn't have the time to screen them at regular speed. At the end of this screening, it was quite clear to me that they were not going to allow this picture to show. But eventually it did. And eventually it showed in the U.K. And of course contemporary films have gone far beyond what we did in *Blood Feast*. But it's like any other groundbreaking proposition — the first one in faces a lot of heat.

We opened the picture in Stan Kohlberg's Bel-Air Drive-In Theater in Peoria, figuring if the film dies in Peoria, who would know? Dave and I both took the pledge that we were not going to go down to that theater to see how the film was doing. But we couldn't stand it. The film opened on a Friday, and by Saturday, we figured the hell with it. We drove down to Peoria. We got about a mile from the theater, and we encountered a pile-up on the highway. I said, "That's all we need, an accident." Well, as it turned out, we were the accident. In one day, the word of mouth regarding this picture had spread to a point where there were not only people out there picketing, saying, "Don't you dare go see this picture," but the place was jammed with cars. There was no room for more cars, and it was truly an exciting event. And at that moment, we both knew we'd struck gold. We didn't quite understand how or why we'd struck gold, but we knew that we had.

And that was when I began planning *Two Thousand Maniacs!*.

For his second foray into the gore genre, H.G. Lewis chose to craft a tale of revenge from beyond the grave titled *Two Thousand Maniacs!*. This time Lewis himself conceived the storyline and crafted the screenplay. Taking a cue from the 1954 Broadway musical *Brigadoon*, the film tells the tale of a Southern town called Pleasant Valley, which reappears a century after the end of the Civil War. Because the town was completely destroyed by Union soldiers, its ghostly citizens seek vengeance against unsuspecting Northerners. They trick their prey into town and convince them that they are the "guests of honor" for their big centennial bash. Then, of course, they kill their guests in a most gruesome manner.

The film, which is Lewis' personal favorite, had a lot of things going for it. The most notable aspect of this film is its impressive production value. For the film's magically-appearing town, Lewis convinced the town of St. Cloud, Florida, to allow him and his crew to shoot extensively there. The town's inhabitants also appear in the film as Pleasant Valley's ghoulish townsfolk. *Two Thousand Maniacs!* also had a bigger budget than *Blood Feast*. This enabled Lewis to cast better actors and spend more time in pre-production.

David Friedman once again insisted that Lewis cast Connie Mason in *Two Thousand Maniacs!*. Despite his extreme unhappiness with her work on *Blood Feast*, Lewis ultimately conceded and cast the young ingénue. Mason would once again try the filmmaker's patience throughout the shoot and this would be the last time she would appear in a Herschell Gordon Lewis picture.

The resulting film was so polished that Lewis would have no problem shopping it as a $500,000 production, despite the fact that its actual budget was less than a tenth of that. *Two Thousand Maniacs!* would have an impressive run theatrically, but would fail to make as much money as its predecessor, *Blood Feast*. Despite this, Lewis — a filmmaker who has always disavowed filmmakers who craft films for the purpose of "art" — would now have his first genuinely respected film in *Two Thousand Maniacs!*.

I don't remember the genesis of *Two Thousand Maniacs!*. I think it came from a casual conversation, which will often give you the best ideas. Then, as we were planning the actual production of *Two Thousand Maniacs!*, we had theaters telling us, "If you made a film that wasn't quite so gross we would play it." And that, of course, was the kingdom of heaven at that time for motion pictures; there were no videocassettes and there were no DVDs then. You either made it in the theaters or not all. And this meant more playing time, so for a film of this type, that was a major factor. In would come a major company product, and that major company would say to the theater, "Okay, here's our deal: we get ninety percent the first two weeks, sixty percent the second two weeks, and then after that it's fifty-fifty." And in we would come with a film like *Blood Feast* and we'd say, "Here's our deal: 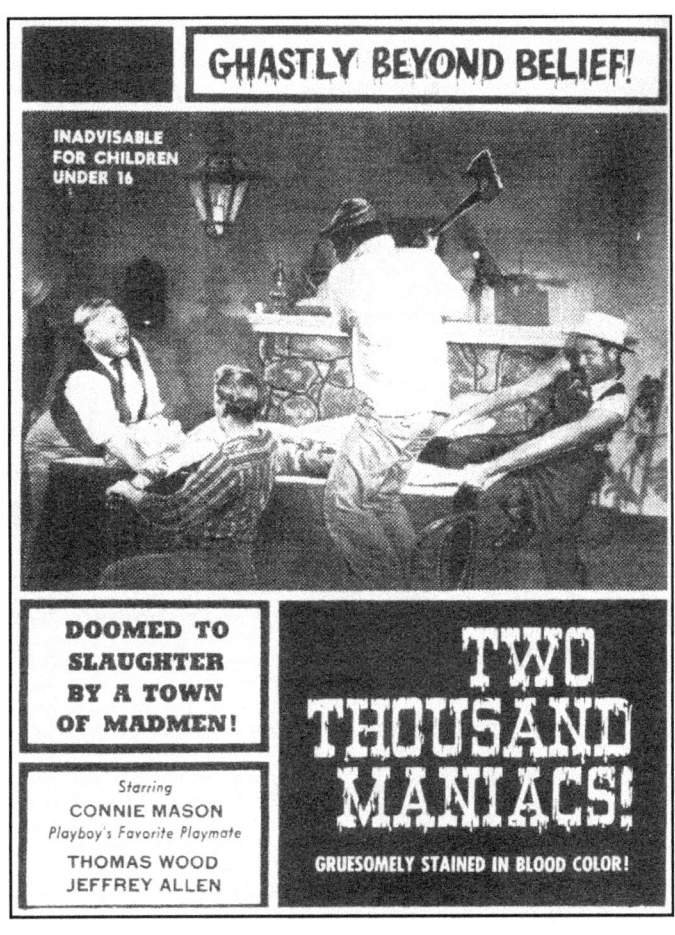 give us thirty-five percent the first week. If the film runs a second week, we'll argue with you then." The theater owner would then think, if I play this film to a half-empty house, I'll still make more money. So the decision was a business decision rather than an artistic one. And one reason so many would-be filmmakers fail in the film business is because they regard it as an art form rather than a business.

First off, *Two Thousand Maniacs!* is my favorite of all the films I made.

I went down to St. Cloud, Florida, which had been recommended to me as a possible location. I was promptly greeted by the mayor, and I was torn. Usually whenever someone asked us what we were going to shoot, our automatic answer would be, "An orange juice commercial." But in this instance I said it was going to be a Civil War story. I took a chance and told them that because St. Cloud was a retirement village, and many of the retirees there were old-timers from southern states. The beauty and logic made this location ideal. I had no problem whatsoever getting the okay to shoot this movie there. Once we had their permission, we just let the thing fly.

We shot that movie with more than double the budget we'd had on *Blood Feast*. The city of St. Cloud gave us a cherry-picker to use on the film, which was a tremendous help. They were extremely helpful. In fact, there was one scene — featuring that huge rock, which was papier-mâché but still weighed about 300 pounds — in which shadows began to creep across the rock as the day wore on. We didn't know what to do about this, but the fellow who had been assigned to assist us said, "No problem." He then assembled a crew and hat racked the trees which were causing the shadows across our set! This was by far and away the most cooperation I had ever had on a picture. And everybody who was out on the street on that Sunday afternoon was an extra in the crowd scene on the main street. My original title had been *Five Thousand Maniacs!*, but there weren't that many people in St. Cloud so I'd had to downgrade the title to *Two Thousand Maniacs!*. Each person who appeared as an extra in that scene was paid with a hamburger. That was actually a mistake on my part because the crew and the cast had gobbled down the food I bought for the extras. So here were these people who had spent all day standing out in the sun, and all they got was a hamburger. But that's showbiz.

On that movie I had a fellow named Taalkius "Talky" Blank, who used the stage name Jeffrey Allen. Taalkius Blank soon became another fixture in our filmmaking group. He would ultimately appear in five or six of my films, and he appeared as the mayor in *Two Thousand Maniacs!*. He was an older fellow who lived in a western suburb of Chicago, and was in fact giving classes in acting — something that many of our cast members could have used. He set the standard for people to live up to on the set. He was always on time, knew all of his lines, delivered them with gusto, and never said, "What kind of movie is this you guys are making?" It's always a pleasure to have someone like that in a key role in a movie.

With some degree of diffidence we had Connie Mason return to play the ingénue. Finally, at one point during the production, it became very clear that she absolutely could not deliver all the lines we had given her. So we gave many of her lines to other people — usually to Bill Kerwin, who played her social partner in the movie. If we hadn't done this, we would have been way over budget for no good reason. The one thing I can say about Connie

Mason is that she was consistent — she was always late and she never knew her lines. On top of this, her lines were not delivered with any sort of validity; they were always delivered as simple recitation.

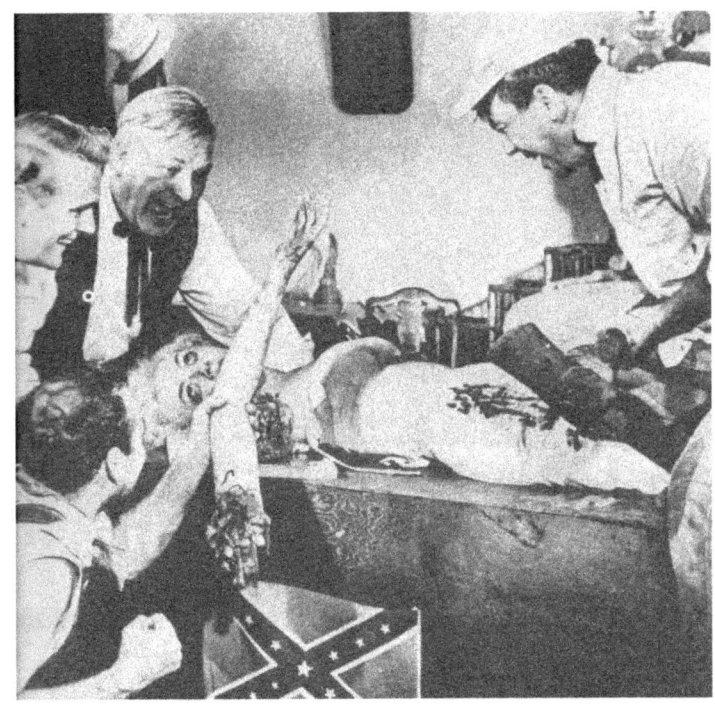

Vincent Santo, who played the child, knew his lines. This was his first movie and we had cast him only because of his size. A couple of years ago, Jimmy Maslon restaged all of this in St. Cloud. And there I met an adult Vincent Santo, not only a grown man but now in middle age. I would never have recognized him, and seeing him now fully-grown made me feel quite old.

We strung our banner across the main street in St. Cloud. It said "PLEASANT VALLEY CENTENNIAL, 1863–1963." One day we were standing outside the hotel and there were two older gentlemen staring at the sign we had hung across the street. And one of the men said, "I wonder why this Pleasant Valley is having its centennial here." And then the other guy said, "I don't think it's the right year, either."

When it came time to record the music for the film, I had this musical group, and they were quite good. They had two guitars and a banjo. A man named Paul Champion played the banjo, and he was absolutely as accomplished a banjoist as I have ever seen in my life. The problem we ran into with the musical group was that they were supposed to sing the theme song for the film, which I had written. We had the entire cast and crew together for an evening to do the rebel yell in the theme, which was titled "The South's Gonna Rise Again." And the group came in to do the song, but the lead singer's voice was too high. There was nothing macho about the way that song was presented. Meanwhile, we'd been shooting all day, and I had the cast and crew present. They had agreed to do this ahead of time, but now they were furious I had dragged them here for this. They weren't going to back out, but they were in no way happy about having to wait for this group to perform the song. I could see that the resentment was growing, so I decided I had to do something quickly. Since I had written the song and since I knew the tempo, I said I would perform it. So, that's my voice singing that song — with no screen credit, I might add — on the sound track of *Two Thousand Maniacs!*. And that little factoid has apparently been noted in history. To this day, whenever I go to a horror film festival, people ask me to sing the theme from *Two Thousand Maniacs!*. And I am always glad to oblige them because I still know every word to that song.

Herschell Gordon Lewis's novelization of his own film *Two Thousand Maniacs!*

Two Thousand Maniacs! never did quite the business *Blood Feast* had. What it did accomplish was that it brought into orbit theaters that would not have played other movies of our type. *Blood Feast* had simply been too primitive for some theaters to risk playing. *Two Thousand Maniacs!*, which had just a touch of historicity to it, and enough production value that it didn't look like someone had made it in a basement, opened a door for the other movies of this type which were to come. It was actually *Two Thousand Maniacs!* more than *Blood Feast* that made this type of movie legitimate.

The 1965 film *Color Me Blood Red* would conclude Herschell Gordon Lewis and David Friedman's "Blood Trilogy," as well as their partnership. Despite the best of intentions, this one, about a mad painter who uses human blood as paint, would be the weakest film of the three. "It definitely was not one of our major pictures," Lewis has said. "We just didn't have our hearts in that one in quite the same way. The effects are not as good. It eventually did all right from a business standpoint, but it was no *Blood Feast*."

Lewis and company shot *Color Me Blood Red* in Sarasota, Florida. The film's skeleton crew consisted of only five people: Lewis and Friedman, as well as actors Gordon Oas-Heim, Jerome Green, and Scott Hall. One Lewis-devised gore scene that did not make the finished film involved a body being chopped up by a boat motor. The problem? Whenever Lewis' crew would throw the pieces of meat into the water, hungry seagulls would immediately scoop them up. Ultimately realizing that he wasn't going to get anything other than shots of seagulls swooping in for the meat, Lewis gave up on capturing this particular scene.

The film would ultimately be the least effective of Lewis' gore pictures primarily because the gore effects weren't up to par with those found in his other films. Lewis himself has stated that it's his own personal least favorite of his gore pictures.

The third film in what has become known as our "Blood Trilogy" was *Color Me Blood Red*. It was about a mad painter who gets his proper red colors from using human blood. Bill Harris, who had previously played the sheriff in *Two Thousand Maniacs!*, suggested an actor for the lead named Gordon Oas-Heim (who appeared under the name Don Joseph). The character he played in *Color Me Blood Red* was Adam Sorg, and subsequent to this, Gordon Oas-Heim used the name Adam Sorg as a screen name. He proved to be an extremely difficult person to work with. His ego was always on the line. He always wanted to rewrite the script, and he always wanted to reinterpret the delivery of lines. There are times when one welcomes that, but not when you're on the kind of schedule we had. Where *Two Thousand Maniacs!* had leaned slightly towards the extensive in production, *Color Me Blood Red* was intensive in that most of the scenes took place inside in either the character's home or studio.

Years later Gordon Oas-Heim appeared on the stage in stock companies around the Chicago area. I was handling publicity for the O'Hare Inn Theater, and who do you suppose was starring in this play alongside the widow of Errol Flynn? Gordon Oas-Heim! And I had the responsibility of handling publicity for that . . . If that isn't the test of someone's professionalism, I don't know what is.

We shot *Color Me Blood Red* before we had received any results from the previous film. One of the problems we had is that we'd made a deal with Stan Kohlberg and another gentleman named Sidney Reich, who was the fourth partner in our company that produced those films. Kohlberg told us he was making a deal with the Exchange Bank in Chicago to form a permanent production company, and therefore we had to build up some sort of a treasury, which is why we were going to hold back distribution of funds from

Blood Feast and *Two Thousand Maniacs!*. So here we were shooting *Color Me Blood Red* on a bare-bones level in Sarasota, and we had a problem with the sound of the waves rocking back and forth. That really knocked the daylights out of our soundtrack. But that was where we were and that was what we did. At the end of this episode, Kohlberg had not released the money from distribution, saying the Exchange Bank was still considering. One day I ran into a fellow named Ted Melin who worked at the bank and I asked, "How are we doing on our film deal?" And he said, "There's no film deal. Kohlberg said, 'Forget it.' " At that point, the three of us — Sidney Reich, Dave Friedman, and myself — sued Stan Kohlberg. There was nothing else to do. He was literally laughing at the whole thing. "Yeah, yeah, it'll all work out." It was typical for Kohlberg, for whom I never had much regard as anything more than a rather oblique business head. As that progressed, Sidney Reich died, and his kids wanted no part of any of this. Whether or not they settled with

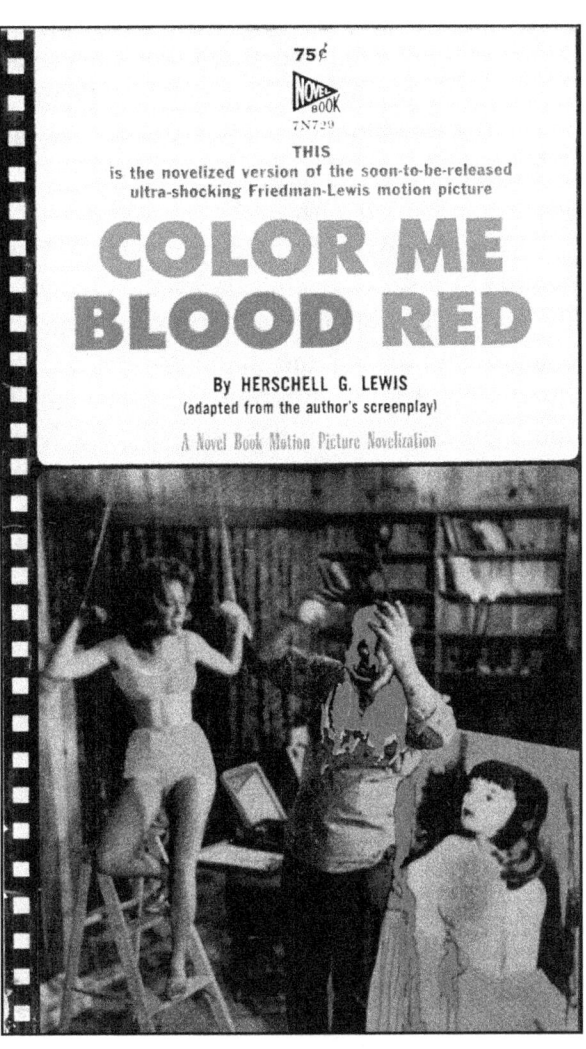

The cover to the paperback novelization of Lewis's film *Color Me Blood Red*.

Kohlberg I'll never know. Then Dave settled unilaterally with Kohlberg without telling me, and then moved to California. So now I was the sole plaintiff in this lawsuit against Stan Kohlberg, which ultimately took two years to settle. And although I wasn't thrilled with the settlement, at least I got one.

I was horrified to lose Dave. I couldn't believe it. His phone was still connected and he had never informed me that any of this was happening. I called repeatedly and there was never an answer. I remember thinking, My God, I hope Dave and Carol, his wife, hadn't died of monoxide poisoning or something. I had no idea what had happened. Then, finally, someone who knew all of us and knew that I had been searching for Dave volunteered this information. "Didn't you know he moved to California to go into business with Dan Sonney?" I knew Dan Sonney — he was in the exploitation film business out there. I said, "Come on!" And the man said, "No, I'm telling you, Dave Friedman settled with Kohlberg and has moved to California. He's gone."

There were two years during which Dave and I did not exchange a word. We didn't talk. I couldn't believe I'd been betrayed in this way. Then, after two years, we ran into each other at the theater owners' convention. We then hugged and kissed and made up, and we were friends right up until Dave's death. I found it interesting that Dave admits in his own book that what he did was rather cowardly. I guess Dave had economic pressures that were beyond mine. Filmmaking was all Dave had to live on, and I always had the advertising business to fall back on.

But during all the turmoil with Sidney Reich and Stan Kohlberg, we made *Color Me Blood Red*, which Dave finished cutting himself. And Bob Sinise, the father of actor Gary Sinise, served as the editor on the film and cut the picture with Dave. There were aspects to this to which I objected, but I figured since we knew the group was splitting up, to heck with it.

Moonshine Mountain — Monster A-Go-Go — Sin, Suffer, and Repent

"Bill Rebane was the original director, writer, producer, and everything else on Terror at Halfday *[later retitled* Monster A-Go-Go*]... I felt that, with 80,000 feet of film to work with, there had to be a movie there somewhere. I was wrong."*

—Herschell Gordon Lewis

With David Friedman out of the picture, Lewis would be forced to make his next film, *Moonshine Mountain*, by himself. However, he was now low on cash. He went to a loyal distributor with whom he had worked with previously named Harry Kerr, and explained his situation. Kerr was excited about this film that Lewis described as being similar to *Thunder Road* with "some comedy in it" and "a little bit of gore." Kerr immediately cut Lewis a check for $8,000, an amount which would cover everything except film processing lab costs.

The film, which has also been shown under the title *White Trash on Moonshine Mountain*, was written by Charles Glore, who also appears in the film as an actor under the name Chuck Scott. The film contained many original country-western songs, most of which were written by Lewis himself. Interestingly, his credit tag on the film read, "Directed by Herschell Gordon Lewis, who ought to know better, but don't."

Distributor Harry Kerr was pleased with the final film, but suggested that it be accompanied by a second feature which they would also control. With no money left to make a second film, Lewis rented the 1959 Paramount film *Li'l Abner* for a mere $15 a day. In the end, *Moonshine Mountain* made a respectable amount of money for Lewis and Kerr and enjoyed a good long theatrical run. "I could never complain about the box-office results of that film," Lewis has said.

Moonshine Mountain was a film that Dave Friedman and I had planned to make when we were suing Stan Kohlberg. We rushed into production because the money was tied up in the other three splatter movies — *Blood Feast*, *Two Thousand Maniacs!*, and *Color Me Blood Red*. Knowing the Chicago court system — and this was quite accurate — we felt it would be quite a while before anyone would even hear the case.

We set this film up with our distributor out of Charlotte, North Carolina, whose name was Harry Kerr. He owned a company called Dominant Pictures of the Carolinas. Harry had always been a very dependable distributor for us on previous movies, and he ordinarily handled the Charlotte, Atlanta, and Jacksonville exchange areas, which were highly significant at that time for any producer of schlock movies.

So off we went into pre-production on *Moonshine Mountain*, and suddenly Dave disappeared. And that was the end. That was when he and I split up. As I stated in the previous chapter, he settled unilaterally with Stan Kohlberg and then relocated to California. So here I was left alone to make *Moonshine Mountain*. Fortunately for me, Harry Kerr was very much interested in this picture. In fact, the whole thing had been his idea to start with. He said he wanted a picture on the order of *Thunder Road*, but with a little bit of blood in it and also some nice music. That was easy for me. I wrote the songs for *Moonshine Mountain*, and that proved to be an easier task than I had become accustomed to. After scoring movies like *Blood Feast*, it was a cakewalk. It had been my plan to compose the music from the moment we first started planning this movie. One of the things Harry Kerr had insisted on was that the film feature hillbilly music. Well, where was I going to find hillbilly music? I wasn't about to pay for the rights to anything, and that was a driving force for me. So I wrote the songs myself.

We shot the film in a place called Bullock Creek, South Carolina, which was about an hour-and-a-half drive away from Charlotte. We set up in a motel in a town called Sharon, South Carolina. If you can imagine Sharon as being the largest town in the area, then you'll have a pretty good idea of what Bullock Creek was like. To put the thing together I brought back some of the old retainers like Ben Moore, who had been one of the highlights of *Two Thousand Maniacs!*. I had Taalkius Blank, using the name Jeffrey Allen, who was pretty much the father of the group. There was also Chuck Scott, whose

real name was Charles Glore, and he played the male lead. He was a guitar player, and a very good one. He had been one of the Pleasant Valley boys in *Two Thousand Maniacs!*. So these were by and large people I had worked with before. And I had Gordon Oas-Heim again.

We built a still that looked big enough that it could probably turn out as much booze as Hiram Walker could produce in a year. It was about fifteen feet high and ten feet in diameter. It was a monstrous thing, made out of metal. We painted it red and placed it on a hillside. Everybody who saw it wondered if it was real. Of course it wasn't real — it was hollow inside. That became another major prop for *Moonshine Mountain*.

In retrospect, I think we shot that film a little too fast. For example, there was a fellow named Harry Hoffman who played the big buffoon. He was a very big fellow, and we had a tough time locating overalls for him. And that came back to haunt me later on, because there's a scene near the end of the film where we blow up that still and he was supposed to be lying there beneath it. And I said, "Let's stuff the overalls with straw or something so we can sit that beneath the still." They couldn't find it. Harry had gone home, and he had taken the overalls with him. So in that one shot in the film, it's naked there; even though he had been lying underneath the thing, there's nothing there in that shot. No one ever called me out on that, by the way. But to this day, even after all these years, it really bothers me that we had to shoot that scene the way we did.

The other problem I had was that we lip-synced the pre-recorded song "My Pappy Built a Still on a Clearing on the Hill." This was supposed to be at a sort of barbecue/feast. Taalkius Blank — Jeffrey Allen — did not know his words. I had them written on a board so he could read them. When it came shooting time, we had a crowd in there. I had learned long before that if you have a crowd, you shoot. You're never going to match it up again. And Taalkius couldn't remember the words, and couldn't read the board. So he visibly mumbles a bit there. But his lips didn't match what he was saying at all! Once again, I should have used reaction shots there, but I didn't have enough of them. And once again, nobody has ever called me on that.

One night Gordon Oas-Heim wandered into my motel room, and he was completely drunk. He came in just slobbering around, and he tried to hit me, but he couldn't because he was so far gone. I think he was angry because we wouldn't expand his role in such a way as he wanted us to. Anyway, I shoved him into a wall, and the walls in that motel were so thin that he left his impression. He then went stumbling out and started annoying other people, and not just our group. Then the police came. And let me tell you, the South Carolina police officers from around Sharon were not about to put up with a bunch of trouble-causing Yankees. They grabbed Gordon Oas-Heim and stuck him in jail. I then went and tried to get him out of jail, which I really didn't want to do. He had already performed most of his part. He only had a couple of lines left to do, and we had decided to scrap them altogether. It just made no sense to have him hanging around any more than he had to. I went to try and get him out of the hoosegow, and these cops were not about to be mollified. They said, "Do you want to join him?" I said, "No, officer, I really don't want to come in there and join him. I just want you to make it possible for me to get him out of your way." The next morning I got him out and off he went. And that concluded my relationship with him. He was a very good actor, but who needs that kind of actor? Every single person in the cast was in favor of us getting rid of him, and we did.

We opened that picture several times. We had a number of "world premieres." Harry was very good with these so-called "world premieres." We had one in Charlotte. We had one in Atlanta. I can't remember where they all were held, but there were a number of these world premieres. The world premiere in Charlotte bothered me immensely. I was sitting there, and people came filtering into this drive-in theater, and there were a bunch of children. It seemed that every other car had children in it, and there was stuff in *Moonshine Mountain* that was not aimed at children; primarily the bloody stuff, which wasn't nearly as gory as what we had shown in our previous films. But I felt very much ill at ease with children watching that. So I got up and went up to the projection room and chopped several pieces of

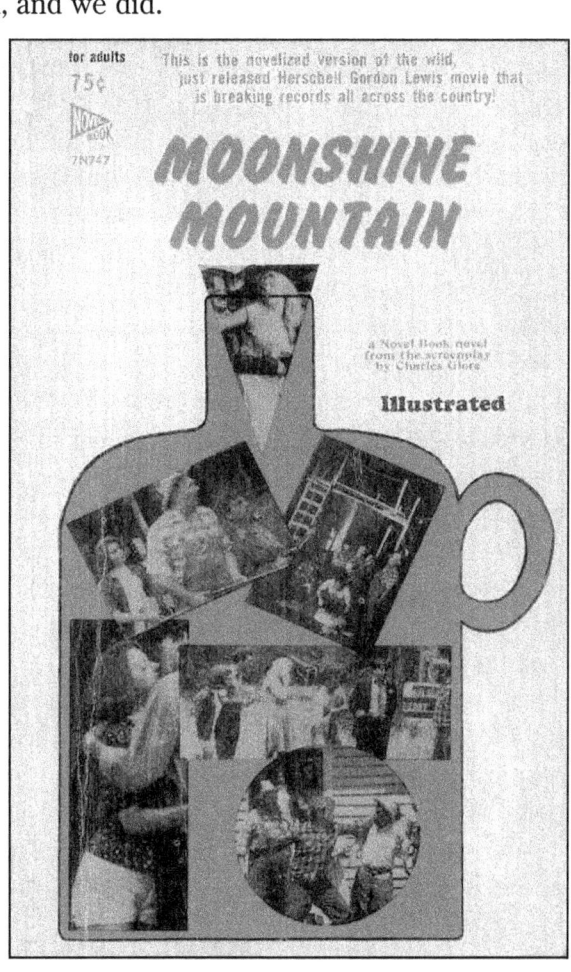

The cover of Herschell Gordon Lewis's novelization of his film *Moonshine Mountain*.

the film out, intending to replace those scenes later. That's why that picture opened with a truncated version. Later on, the projectionist said he put the scenes back in. Whether or not he actually did, I have no idea.

Moonshine Mountain supported me for a good two years. I have absolutely no complaints about that picture. Some of the theater chains would take an old, beat-up print and then make a deal where they could use that print for six months in any way they wanted to use it. I was just sort of bicycling it around from theater to theater. You can imagine the condition of that print by the time its run was complete. To bring the story to a logical conclusion, we lost that picture. Somehow or another, the negative vanished. Then, a few years back, I received a phone call from Harry Kerr, who had tracked me down. He said he was retiring and that he had located a print of *Moonshine Mountain* that was in good condition. I had been scouring the universe trying to find a print of that film for some time, and had no luck at all. He said, "I have one. What do I do with it?" I said, "Harry, you run — don't walk — to the nearest post office and send that print to Jimmy Maslon. About two weeks later I got a call from Jimmy, just laughing his head off. He said, "Why did you send me a junk print?" I said, "Jimmy, it may be a junk print, but it's the last one in existence, as far as I know." He said it was too far gone to clean up, but that he'd "do something." And sure enough, he put some sort of scratch remover on that thing, and now *Moonshine Mountain* exists in a second incarnation. It's not in great shape, but it exists.

Monster-A-Go-Go is a different breed of Herschell Gordon Lewis film, in that it is not really a Herschell Gordon Lewis film at all. The film was begun by filmmaker Bill Rebane, who also helmed 1975's *The Giant Spider Invasion*. Rebane worked on the film for more than two years. However, he eventually ran out of funds and had to shut down production. His film was then seized by the laboratory when Rebane was unable to pay for its processing.

Enter Herschell Gordon Lewis. Hoping to edit it into a coherent film he could use as the second part of a double bill with his own *Moonshine Mountain*, Lewis purchased Rebane's film. However, Lewis soon found that he could not edit the existing footage into a film that made any sort of sense. He then shot new footage and added narration, making something completely different out of Rebane's film.

The resulting film is crude, but ultimately did what it was intended to do. Lewis takes no credit for the film, and has never considered it one of his own. Because it is often (erroneously) credited as being a Herschell Gordon Lewis film, the filmmaker discusses the misguided film's bastardly creation here.

Monster-A-Go-Go has a unique history. The movie was begun by a fellow named Bill Rebane. I had known Bill when I was over at United Film and Recording Studio in Chicago. He was a German immigrant who had come to the United States to learn the movie business. One thing that was notable about Bill Rebane was that he had a notion regarding a process that was very much like Cinerama, which he dubbed Cinetarium. So Bill decided to make a movie . . . Well, everyone wants to make a movie, and everyone thinks he can do it, but actually being able to do this is a completely different story.

Bill Rebane then hired some fairly well-known second-tier actors to appear in this movie. He started shooting, but then faced some desertion because he ran out of money in the middle of the shoot. He then came to me and asked me to be his cinematographer to shoot some footage at night on Wacker Drive in Chicago. Like a moron, I said, "Okay, I'll do it." I guess I felt some compassion for a guy who had started a movie and couldn't finish it. We also did some shooting in Lincoln Park.

In this movie, Bill Rebane featured an extremely tall fellow named Henry Hite. He had previously been a part of an old vaudeville act called Low, Hite & Stanley. As you might imagine, "Low" had been a midget. Hite had, of course, been Henry Hite, who was then billing himself as The World's Tallest Man — he was about seven-and-a-half feet tall — and Stanley was just an ordinary guy. And what a strange act this was! When Stanley — the ordinary guy — left the act, they disbanded. I find this funny considering that Stanley would have easily been the most replaceable member of the act! Henry Hite was living in a hotel room on Rush Street in Chicago, and was really down on his luck. His physical condition was not too good at that time, either. His ankles had reached a point where they would no longer support his weight. It was very difficult for him to walk due to his size and lack of physical condition. He was a charming chap, and was always looking back fondly at the "good old days" in which he and his two partners had been able to stand on stage and perform their act.

The whole idea of *Monster-A-Go-Go* was that an astronaut travels into space and becomes irradiated. Then, when he returns to earth, he looks like a monster. Bill Rebane's original title for this film had been *Terror at Halfday*, which refers to a small town called Halfday located about forty-five miles outside Chicago. Of course, nobody knows that, so why he gave the film that title I'll never know.

We shot this movie over a long period of time. I was his cameraman on two occasions. Then there were other people shooting for him on other occasions. It was almost like a joke. Whenever he would have a little money, he would shoot some more of the film. Then, when he ran out of money, they would stop again. And one of the main penalties of shooting in this manner was that he would lose cast and crew members as he went along. One of the funniest things that happened during filming involved an actor who began the film as a bald man. Then he eventually bought a hairpiece, and Bill just went on filming him, but now with the hair. No one seemed to think anything about it! So in part of the movie the guy is bald, and in part of the movie he has a hairpiece. There's no sequence to it.

Eventually Bill Rebane ran out of money, and the laboratory took this negative — filmed in glorious black-and-white, by the way — and locked it away. So when I was trying to put together the second half of a double bill with *Moonshine Mountain*, a representative of the laboratory told me, "I've got one of your films here." I said, "What do you mean?" He said, "Well, I know you were involved with it. It's this thing called *Terror at Halfday*." I thought, oh, boy! I asked him what he had, and the guy said he had 80,000 feet of film. Can you imagine that? Eighty thousand feet of film? That's 10 times the raw stock we used to film *The Adventures of Lucky Pierre*! So I said, "Okay, send it to me." So he sent it to me, and what a mistake I made there!

I soon found that two things had happened. First, they had cut the slates off, so I had to sync the whole film up by eye. I actually had a cutter at that time. His name was Dick Brinkman, and old Dick hated to come to work each day when he had to cut this thing. The other problem was that the movie made absolutely no sense at all. Despite its having 80,000 feet of film, the footage had no sign of a story anywhere to be found. So I went out and shot a thousand feet of telegrams, feet walking, hands gesticulating, in the hopes of making a coherent movie out of it. Bill Rebane had been deadly serious with his movie, but I knew it had to be regarded as a satire.

My name is not on *Monster-A-Go-Go*. It is known throughout the industry that I finished the film, but I still contend that it is not my movie. I retitled it and advertised it with the tagline "An astronaut went up, a you know what came down." I then used it as the second half of the double bill with *Moonshine Mountain*.

Years and years later — long after I had forgotten this peccadillo — I got a call from Bill Rebane. He told me that Turner Classic Movies wanted to show *Monster-A-Go-Go*! And I said, "Don't you have some pictures of your kids? They'd do much better showing those." I just couldn't believe it. Bill then got into a huge argument with a man named Jeff Hogue. I was familiar with Jeff Hogue because he had purchased a movie made by Pat Patterson called *Doctor Gore*. And Patterson was the number two man in Harry Kerr's office in the Carolinas. He had been exposed to this kind of movie, and he felt like everybody else — if they can make one, I can make one. So Jeff Hogue had purchased this movie, *Doctor Gore*, after Pat Patterson died. He then asked me to film an introduction to the film, which I did. (I have still never seen *Doctor Gore*, even at this late date. But that's of no consequence; Pat Patterson was a good guy, and I've always felt that good guys deserve as much help as the rest of us good guys can give him.) Jeff Hogue then became enamored with the movie business, and years later had picked up the rights to *Monster-A-Go-Go*. I didn't care one way or the other. I had long since forgotten that the movie even existed. As far as I knew, Jimmy Maslon owned that picture since he had purchased the rights to all my other films. So I just let all of them argue it out. Again, I didn't care one way or the other.

So I was traveling in West Africa, and I got a call on my cell phone. It was Bill Rebane asking me to back him up in his argument with Jeff Hogue because he felt he had creative rights to *Monster-A-Go-Go*. I said, "Bill, if there's such a thing as creative rights to a movie that was seized on a laboratory lien, I don't know what that is." So it's all up in the air right now; nobody seems to know who actually owns the rights to *Monster-A-Go-Go*. I hope whoever owns it takes a look at the movie before deciding to pursue any expense with it, because it's as bad as a movie can possibly be.

A friend of Herschell Gordon Lewis' purchased an information reel about venereal disease. Hoping to transform this into some sort of exploitation film, he enlisted Lewis' talents. Lewis filmed new footage, edited in footage similar to *Mom and Dad*, and added a narrative track, transforming the venereal disease film into a film purporting to show the dangers of out-of-wedlock pregnancy. The film was then titled *Sin, Suffer and Repent*.

Like *Monster-A-Go-Go*, this is not a Herschell Gordon Lewis film. However, due to inaccurate attributions and erroneous filmographies, Lewis has chosen to explain his participation in the project here.

Sin, Suffer and Repent was owned by a fellow from Toledo, Ohio. He had purchased a World War II venereal disease picture and decided to transform it into a "birth of a baby" picture like *Mom and Dad*. In the world of exploitation movies at that time, some of the weird stuff about marijuana and what have you, was getting playing time where conventional pictures were not. And he bought this film for next to nothing. I mean, who wanted a World War II sex disease movie? So we looked at this thing, and he decided to make it "birth of a baby." So I went over to Weiss Hospital in Chicago, and put some girl on a gurney, and built up her belly to almost grotesque proportions. I thought it turned out to be quite funny, but he didn't think it was funny, and he got a lot of playing time out of it.

My name is intentionally not present on that film. I never even considered putting my name on that movie, and I really don't like that some people believe I directed it. All I did was add some footage to transform it from a venereal disease movie into a "birth of a baby" picture. I do know that it screened for some time, and now I get the blame for it.

An Eye for an Eye –
Jimmy the Boy Wonder – The Magic Land of Mother Goose

"People look at Jimmy the Boy Wonder *today and they don't appreciate — and they have no reason to appreciate — how it was made. But at the time, within the industry, to have a movie like that which had actual animation in it, lifted our movie well above all the other cheap schlock stuff that was out there."*

—Herschell Gordon Lewis

In the 1960s, a would-be producer approached Herschell Gordon Lewis about making a film. Lewis agreed to film and direct the project, which was to be titled *An Eye for an Eye*. The film, which Lewis says "wasn't bad," featured Bill Kerwin as a blind man who receives an eye transplant.

"It was about a man who wills his eyes to whoever can get them," Lewis explained to *Godfather of Gore* author Randy Palmer. "It then turns out that his eyes have special powers. He was actually part of a group that planned to take over the world, and his only way of getting out was to kill himself in an automobile crash and have his eyes go to somebody else who might then be able to break up this unholy ring."

Unfortunately, funding would ultimately fall through, effectively putting the kibosh on the film before it was finished. Jimmy Maslon, who has restored and re-released many of Lewis' films, owns an unedited negative of the existing footage, but there are no plans to release *An Eye for an Eye* at this time.

An Eye for an Eye is significant because it is the only film Herschell Gordon Lewis has not finished.

An Eye for an Eye was a movie that I really wasn't too excited about making. It was a jinxed shooting to start with. There was a man who worked in my office named Paul Hunter. Paul wanted to be involved with movie production, so we used poor Paul's car for a shot. Theoretically there was a man standing in the middle of the road, and the car runs into this guy and kills him. We had a dummy standing in the middle of the road, and Paul drove his car smack into that dummy. The head came off and went right through the windshield of his car! We had to have his car towed away. Meanwhile, he was shooting dozens of still photographs because he said his car was a "star" of this movie, which never came to be.

The backing for the picture disappeared as we started to shoot. It was a very strange situation there. Then somehow the negative for this film ended up in the hands of a man named Abbott Schwartz, who was a distributor from Minneapolis. Abbott Schwartz said, "Don't worry about it. I'm going to finish this movie." Years passed and I forgot about it until Jimmy Maslon ended up with the film. It has never been fully cut, but I see there's footage in Jimmy's documentary. But the movie was never completed.

No one could have predicted what Herschell Gordon Lewis, the filmmaker responsible for the birth of the splatter genre, would do next — a live-action children's film!

The film, made for a producer named Hal Berg, would feature Berg's wife, Jo Ann Berg. The project would be titled *Jimmy the Boy Wonder*, and would tell the story of a boy who learns that he can stop time whenever he wants. Making the film even more interesting, Lewis secured the rights to a 1952 French cartoon entitled *The Curious Adventures of Mr. Wonderbird*. In an effort to give *Jimmy the Boy Wonder* added production value, Lewis then edited in animated scenes from the French film, making his movie one of the first films to feature both live-action and animation.

The resulting film is a bizarre offering on par with any of Lewis' more adult-themed films. A reviewer for the website Kiddie Matinee describes *Jimmy the Boy Wonder* as featuring "amateur-night acting, loud psychedelic fashions, some crazy songs, utterly tacky photography, myriad occult overtones, scary characters, evil incantions, etc." The reviewer goes on to say that the film "thus comes across like some sort of evil LSD home movie for kids, like *The Wizard of Oz* as remade by Kenneth Anger."

Hal Berg's wife, Jo Ann Berg, had a children's television program in Chicago. Hal Berg wanted to put his wife in the movies. He wanted her to be a star, and he wanted it to be a children's movie. That was all that mattered to him. And he was going to finance it, which was very dear to my heart.

Off we went to Florida, and I brought Larry Wellington with me. There was no real plotline, so I had to come up with one. The plot I came up with was about a child who was able to stop time. In keeping with the classic children's story, there had to be a heavy. We knew a fellow named David Blight, and we gave him the title Mr. Fig — the evil creature in *Jimmy the Boy Wonder*. He was always trying to foil Jimmy and whatever he was trying to do.

Jimmy would just yell out, "I want time to stop!" The master clock would stop because he yelled that out, which meant that everything came to a halt. I didn't have any kind of budget there, because Hal Berg's notion of budget was even worse than mine. But I got to go to Florida, so I wasn't going to argue that his budget was insufficient. So when Jimmy stops time, we would simply have people who were moving stop moving. And it was moderately okay. One of the people was Bill Kerwin, pushing a lawn mower. One of the actors couldn't stay still. But that was okay.

It didn't matter. This wasn't that type of movie anyway. There was another trick where Jimmy turned the whole world red. All I did was stick a red filter in the camera.

We shot sequences at a place called Coral Castle in Miami. It was built by someone as a monument to his wife. It was constructed from stone. Doris Wishman had also shot a picture there called *Nude on the Moon*. Coral Castle really looks like another planet. It looks like you're on another landscape. There's nothing there but these stone buildings. We used that location because I wanted it to look unworldly. That worked very, very well.

We utilized one rolling shot in Coral Castle. I simply sat in a wheelbarrow with two people pushing it — one on each end — and that's how we achieved our "dolly shot." We didn't have tracks, and we didn't have any other way of pushing that big camera around.

Another peculiarity of *Jimmy the Boy Wonder* is that some French animation became available. It was not in the least bit related to the movie. I convinced Hal Berg to purchase that animation so we could put some production value in the movie. We bought that animation with the French soundtrack, and I then re-recorded a new soundtrack over that. That entire English soundtrack, which included many voices, was performed by three people. I was one of the three. I was the lead on the soundtrack with all kinds of sounds and whistles on it. We had a good time recording that.

Hal Berg distributed this thing originally, and it did good business. One of the advantages to aiming full-on at a particular audience is that you don't have to worry about reviews. You also don't have to worry about people leaving the theater and saying what a cheap piece of crap it was. In this case, the film matched the people who were looking at it, which were children under the age of 10. It was a success because we never had a theater say to us, "Yank that picture out of here."

Years passed by, and I thought *Jimmy the Boy Wonder* was long lost. And then, again, Jimmy Maslon turned up with a print of it. Nothing ever seems to disappear forever in this strange and wonderful movie world.

Pity Herschell Gordon Lewis for once again being blamed for an abominable film project that was not his own. This time the offending project was the children's film *The Magic Land of Mother Goose*. Lewis was approached in 1966 by a man named Jack Baker. Baker produced a local stage production of *The Magic Land of Mother Goose*, and sought to capture the play on film.

"*Mother Goose* was simply a camera job," Lewis has said. "It was a film that was made for someone else, and the producer needed someone who knew how to operate a camera. So I agreed to be the camera operator on that picture."

In the years since the film was released in 1967, Lewis has repeatedly been identified as the writer and director behind the filmed stage play. Because of this, Lewis agreed to clear all of this up for this book.

The film has also been released under the title *Santa Claus Visits The Magic Land of Mother Goose*. Interestingly, surviving copies of the film are missing the wraparound sequences featuring Santa Claus, leaving confused viewers asking why Santa's name appears in the alternate title.

Jack Baker had a troupe of actors to perform *The Magic Land of Mother Goose* on stage. On the weekends — usually a Saturday and a Sunday — in which the movies showing the theater were totally adult, he would make a deal for the matinee. He would substitute his live show for the movie. It worked very well for him. As you can imagine, in that kind of circumstance, the staging had to be relatively primitive, because he had to set it up and tear it down in a big hurry.

So this was a group of actors telling the story of Mother Goose. All I did was supply two cameras, which is a lot of film. But nobody cared, because like most of my movies, there was no take two here. A famous line from that performance was one girl saying, "We'd better stop. The head fell off my sheep!" We simply shot the live performance. We shot it in chunks, but it was the live stage show.

One of the funniest things about that was, we added the beginning and the end later. But when the lab put it together, they put the end of the film at the beginning, and the beginning at the end. Taalkius Blank played Santa Claus, and he was supposed to open and close the film. But as it turned out, the film began with Santa Claus saying, "Wasn't that entertaining, boys and girls?" And the movie ends with, "Boys and girls, I've got a wonderful story to tell you." It was quite funny, and it was no big deal to put it back together the correct way. The only people who saw it in that original incarnation were the group that owned it.

Something Weird – Suburban Roulette – Blast-Off Girls

> *"One problem with* Blast-Off Girls *involved the title. The copyright date on the main title sequence turned out to be so big that it dwarfed the title of the movie . . . We said, as we often did, 'Oh, well, we'll just leave it as is.' "*
>
> —Herschell Gordon Lewis

A collegiate educator named James Hurley came to Herschell Gordon Lewis in early 1966 with a rough idea for a film. He wanted to make a movie that validated the idea of extra-sensory perception, or ESP. Lewis agreed to make the film, and the two men established a company through which to make the film. It was called Hurlew Productions. Lewis agreed to shoot and direct the film, and Hurley agreed to write a screenplay. For the film's title, Lewis revived a title he had conceived some time previously; the title, *Something Weird*, was the original title Lewis had concocted for *Blood Feast* when that film was still in its infancy.

Even in the beginning Lewis could see that the film James Hurley wanted to create would make very little money, so he began reworking scenes and crafted the film into something more commercial. James Hurley distanced himself from the final project and soon began planning a second film on ESP titled *The Psychic*.

James Hurley was a teacher at a school near Chicago called Triton College. Jim Hurley had two fanatical interests. One was movie-making, and the other was extra-sensory perception, or ESP. He was somewhat of a disciple of a fellow named Peter Hurkos, who billed himself as a psychic. Peter Hurkos was, to James Hurley, next to God, or maybe even a little bit in front. Jim absolutely believed whatever Hurkos said, whether he was trying to solve a problem for the police or simply predicting what might happen next. Peter Hurkos could make no mistakes. So, James Hurley wanted to make a film built around the notion that extrasensory perception had great validity to it.

James Hurley wrote the script. I was the cameraman, and I also directed, although James was pretty much the majordomo all the way. I guess you might say I gave technical direction.

Something Weird's plotline was rather primitive, as most of my plotlines are. A man who regards himself as a rather handsome devil becomes disfigured when he loses a fight with an electric wire. And out comes this witch, played by Mudite Arums. She then strikes up a deal with the young man, which is that she will give him back his good looks if he will become her lover. The plot twist was that everyone else saw her as a beautiful woman, but he couldn't. He saw her as the ugly witch. But he was trapped in that situation.

In *Something Weird*, my feeling of achievement came from my accomplishing optical effects without using optical effects. I think we saved somewhere in the neighborhood of $40,000 by doing in the camera what otherwise would have had to be filmed out with the laboratory doing the optical effects. In one scene, we had an actor in a chair back his chair all the way through the wall. How do you do that when you have no money? You do it in the camera, and if it doesn't work, then you scrap that effect. It turned out that it did work.

We put this film together and James Hurley was not pleased with it, because this was not the movie he had intended to make. That was probably true. My feeling, as well as the feelings of people in the world of distribution, was that the movie he intended to make had very little box-office value. Rather, it was an encomium to the whole notion of extra-sensory perception. James Hurley then decided to make his own movie. He did, and he called it *The Psychic*, which you'll read about later in this volume.

Today *Something Weird* has achieved some minor immortality in that Something Weird Video, which now distributes many of my films, takes its name from the film's title.

Herschell Gordon Lewis happened upon a screenplay written by *Living Venus* scribe Jim McGinn. The script, entitled *Suburban Roulette*, focused on wife swapping. Just as he had with *Living Venus*, Lewis heavily rewrote the screenplay, sometimes providing shading, often times clarifying, and at other times just replacing problematic scenes altogether. The film is significant because it was Lewis' first collaboration with producer David Chudnow, who would later assist on *How to Make a Doll* and *Just for the Hell of It*.

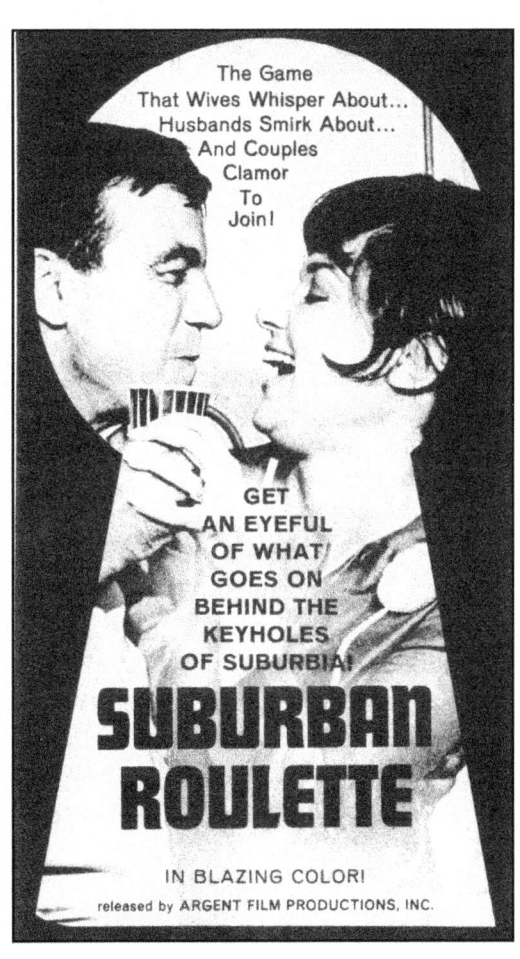

Suburban Roulette follows the Fisher family, newly just moved to the Illinois suburbs in the hopes of escaping Mrs. Fisher's urges to cheat. The couple become friends with several neighborhood couples, and innocent cookouts soon turn into partner-swapping sessions.

Humorously, a title card at the end of the film announces, "This story is fictitious. If you know of any resemblance to any living person, keep your mouth shut!"

This film was about wife-swapping in the suburbs. Over my own better judgment, I brought in Ben Moore. (Ben Moore, as you might remember, had already appeared in *Two Thousand Maniacs!* and *Moonshine Mountain*.) The rest of the cast was comprised of old standbys, as well. Of course we had Bill Kerwin, as well as actresses Ione Rolnick, Elizabeth Wilkinson, and Allison Louise Downe.

There was a fellow named Don Logay, whose family owned a house that was vacant at the time. It was a big house, and it had a pool, and the pool had water in it. He let us shoot there. The problem we had was that it was in a western suburb, near O'Hare Airport in Chicago. We would be shooting a scene, and then a plane would take off. Planes were taking off every thirty seconds or so! As a result, the sound was terrible, but we didn't have to pay for the location. It was a mixed blessing there.

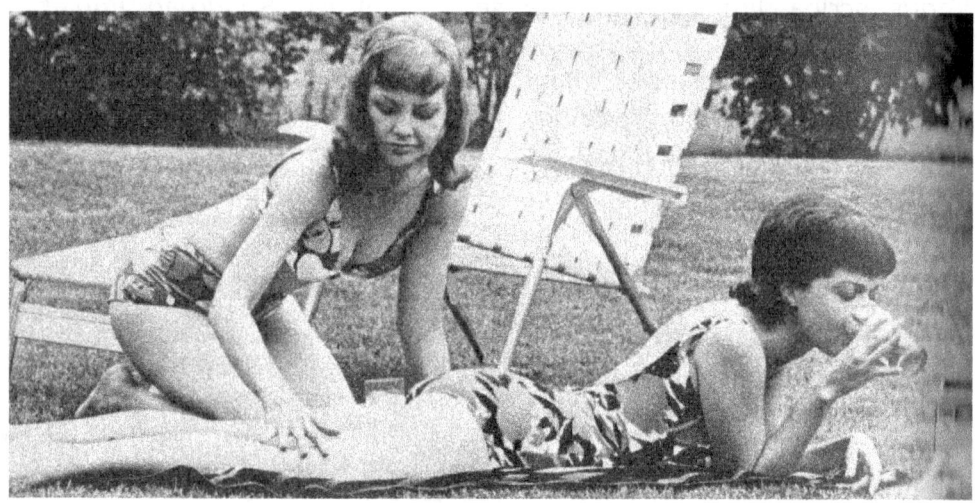

A still from the Herschell Gordon Lewis film *Suburban Roulette*.

We wound up filming a lot of the stuff in the evenings. With the lights we had, try lighting a swimming pool at night, where light flashes and bursts all the time. You've really got to be careful. But there again we got lucky with that.

The shooting had one glitch in it. Allison Louise Downe and Ben Moore got into a really heated argument, and I actually thought at one point they were about to exchange blows. Everyone was gathered around, holding the two of them back, which I found funny. Ben was not a burly guy, but he was pugnacious, and so was she. Despite these kinds of setbacks, the film was finished on time and within the budget.

I was somewhat concerned about the playing of it. I felt it was too much of an in-between; it wasn't hot enough to compete with movies that depended on things like sex or gore, and it wasn't sophisticated enough to compete with conventional movies. It wound up doing pretty well at the box office, which I believe is a testament to the combination of title and campaign. I was fairly proud of that advertising campaign because we did walk a tightrope on that. Also, the reviews were not unfavorable. I think this was partially because the cast was comprised of people I had worked with a number of times previously.

One of the problems we had with *Suburban Roulette* involved a song we recorded for the film. I had a family record "You Are My Sunshine." But then it turned out that someone had a copyright on that song and we couldn't clear it. The result of that was we recorded another song right on top of it, and the lip-syncing didn't work. But nobody seemed to mind that. No one ever said a word about it. I wasn't about to get involved in a lawsuit over that song, which I had always believed was in the public domain.

I have no complaints about *Suburban Roulette*. I'm told that it occasionally still plays here and there, and now they're selling DVDs of it.

Following the success of films like *A Hard Day's Night*, Herschell Gordon Lewis sought to make a rock-and-roll film. "We wanted to cash in on the trend where rock-and-roll groups were really knocking them dead," Lewis recalls. "There hadn't been a movie like that in our budget range, and our budget range made it possible for theater owners to make a deal where they couldn't make a deal with the major companies who demanded too large a percentage. I felt it would be a good business move to make a picture like this." The resulting film would be *Blast-Off Girls*, a rock exploitation vehicle starring Dan Conway, Ray Sager, and Tom Tyrell, as well as a cameo by Kentucky Fried Chicken founder Colonel Harlan Sanders.

The film shines a light on the dark side of the music, focusing on a sleazy record promoter named Boojie Baker (Conway) who enlists the talents of a pop band. He then books performance dates, secures publicity, and lands them a recording contract. The only problem is that he rips off the artists, even going so far as to cause legal troubles for them when they balk at the arrangement.

We shot most of the film in Chicago. We also shot some of it in Cleveland, because the fellow who helped put this thing together had connections there. There was a great line where the girls are in the recording studio and a technician says, "Come on, Baker. We're not shooting X-rays." And that was made up on the spot, I'm pleased to tell you, by me. For about a year after we filmed that, people who were involved with *Blast-Off Girls* kept repeating that line, which to me, was the kingdom of Heaven.

There's an interesting story regarding *Blast-Off Girls*. We always made deals for cast and crew lunches in exchange for shooting scenes somewhere. We did it with Church's Chicken in *Year of the Yahoo!*, and we did it with Kentucky Fried Chicken repeatedly. In this particular instance, we made a deal to shoot for a day at Kentucky Fried Chicken in Wilmette, Illinois. I made the deal with whoever was handling public relations for the franchise. A couple of days before we were about to shoot that scene, I got a call from someone I didn't know identifying himself as a representative of that public relations organization. He said Colonel Harlan Sanders would be in town at the time we were shooting. "What do you think of the idea of him serving fried chicken on camera?" As you can imagine, I jumped at that one. We made the deal, and sure enough, the Colonel showed up with a retinue reminiscent of those that follow the President of the United States.

He had a couple of lines to say, and he rehearsed them and rehearsed them to death. He wanted to rewrite his lines, and the way he wanted to rewrite them would have made no sense at all in terms of plotline. All he had to do was serve chicken to our cast and crew. We started to shoot this thing, and Sanders said, "We must shoot that again." I was about to say, "We're out of film," because we had a good take. Then somebody else said, "Let's just make another rehearsal." And we shot it again, identifying it as a rehearsal. Then we backed out of it, saying, "We have to leave this location. We have enough pieces to put together." Of course we would just pick one take out of it, but he would gladly have shot all day, just repeating that one line over and over again.

In the credits, you will see Colonel Harlan Sanders as a credit. But instead of using his name, we simply showed the iconic cartoon picture of him. I was delighted to have that there.

There was a store on Michigan Avenue in Chicago called George Mashbitz, and George Mashbitz was a custom tailor. We decided to shoot a scene where the film's protagonist outbids his musicians at this custom-fitting store. George Mashbitz's store had a huge, overpowering sign in the window saying, "Feature Film Shooting Here Today!" Who do you think saw that sign? Someone from the union, which we were not utilizing. We were in the middle of shooting, and this guy storms into the store and says in a very loud voice, "You're going to stop shooting!" I knew who he was. I said, "Before you make that kind of pronouncement, I will make one of my own. If we stop shooting you're going to start getting sued for an amount that I don't believe even your union can afford." He just stared at me, and we had this staring contest. Then he stormed out. At this point, George Mashbitz was afraid he might losing some business and said, "Are they going to throw a rock through my window?" I said, "No. These guys have lots of threats but absolutely no guts, and we are absolutely legal or we wouldn't be here." And we were allowed to finish our shot in George Mashbitz's store.

Once again we had sound problems on *Blast-Off Girls*. One of the reasons for this is that we shot a lot of it on location. A second reason is that the device typically used to capture sound for a motion picture, known as a Nagra, was beyond our resources. But we had a device called a Uher, which was a good machine, but not a great one. The difference between a Nagra and a Uher wasn't response; they both had the same response ratio. They both ran in absolute synchronization with twenty-four frames a second on the camera. But the Uher would pick up extraneous sounds somehow that the Nagra did not. The result was that we would often get buzzing or humming sounds. I remember back on *Two Thousand Maniacs!* I had to find a song in the key that the hum came through in which to simply drown out the hum itself. But it wasn't disastrous, even in *Blast-Off Girls*, which was a film that had to have good sound in it.

Blast-Off Girls had a different kind of distribution. Some of the distributors were delighted to get that film because they felt we had been overloading the market with gory movies. And *Blast-Off Girls* filled a niche in that we were able to demand playing time without embarrassing the theater, and we were not demanding a big enough percentage to make it unprofitable for them even if they played to a half-filled house. That was our key anyway. That was always our argument — that if you play our movie, even if your theater is just half-filled, you're gonna make more money than you're gonna get playing a major company film to a full house. And they understood that. The logic was absolute, so the film did quite well in theaters.

The Girl, the Body, and the Pill – A Taste of Blood – The Gruesome Twosome

> *"I regard* A Taste of Blood *as undoubtedly my best picture. I had cooperation on that film that no one has had before or since. It's two hours long and it's heavily produced. You could almost think of it as* Gore with the Wind.*"*
>
> —Herschell Gordon Lewis

Billed as the "first motion picture about the great moral revolution," *The Girl, the Body, and the Pill*, is a minor H.G. Lewis effort. The film tackled the then-controversial subject of birth control.

"*The Girl, the Body, and the Pill* was originally titled simply *The Pill*," Lewis explains. "I made a terrible mistake on that one by announcing that we were in production, figuring that would lock in distribution before we even made the movie. This was a very, very timely film. It was when the birth control pill had just become a major factor. *Variety* came out and announced the completion of a film titled *The Pill*, and it hadn't been titled *The Pill* to start with. I then decided to re-title it *The Girl, the Boy, and the Pill*. And that wouldn't work either. We already had the second campaign put together when we figured that out. In order to get the film out there, we had to change "boy" to "body," so we just inserted a letter in there."

Interestingly, Lewis' actual name appears on the film as producer and director — a rarity on Lewis' sex-related pictures.

The star of this film was a girl named Nancy Lee Noble, and you may recognize that name because she had a beautiful ingénue look to her. She was also in *She-Devils on Wheels* as Honey-Pot. The plot to *The Girl, the Body, and the Pill* was that this girl was stealing her mother's birth control pills and replacing them with simple aspirin. The result of this is that her mother gets pregnant. There's a great line in there — "I'm what?"

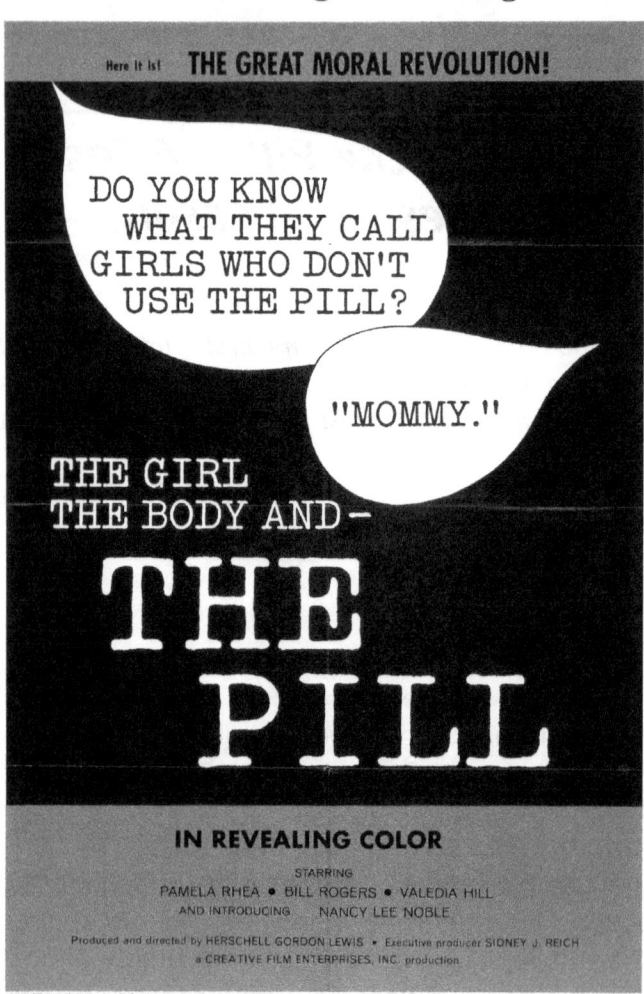

I wrote the theme song for the film, and it became an absolute smash. My old buddy Larry Aberman, who sometimes used the pseudonym Larry Aberwood, fancied himself as a nightclub singer. He really wasn't. He was a would-be actor who worked as a manufacturer of towels. But he was a friend and a neighbor, and he did have a good voice, and he agreed to sing this song, which I wrote. My voice was also one of the four in the barbershop quartet singing the chorus (which, I might point out, was sung to the tune of the Cornell University anthem). It turned out to be a huge hit. We had a lot of luck with that theme song. I was very pleased with that.

This film had a rarity for one of my films, and that was good acting. But that didn't seem to make a lot of difference. *The Girl, the Body, and the Pill* performed adequately at the box office, but it didn't knock them dead the way I had hoped it would. I believe one of the reasons for this is that all of a sudden there was this flood of movies that either peripherally or directly addressed the notion of the birth control pill. That film played second on a double bill with *Blast-Off Girls*, and no one in distribution or exhibition ever asked why we put those two pictures

together. I really didn't want to put those two pictures together. I felt that both of them were worthy of being first-pictures on a double bill. But I didn't have a second feature to go with either one. In both cases because of the timeliness of it, I just felt it was wiser to get the movies out as soon as possible than to wait around for movies to pair them with.

With *A Taste of Blood*, H.G. Lewis made his contribution to the Dracula mythos. For this modern-day Dracula story, Lewis utilized a screenplay by a local screenwriter named Donald Stanford. However, the screenplay was problematic as it was as big as the Chicago phone book and had numerous structural problems. Lewis then reworked the script, which was initially titled *The Secret of Dr. Alucard*, and retitled it *A Taste of Blood*.

At the time he was making the film, Lewis believed it to be just another one of his films. However, the resulting film is easily one of his finest efforts. In fact, most aficionados agree that *A Taste of Blood* is the director's masterwork. That Lewis was able to pass off this $40,000 film as a $400,000 film to distributors stands as a testament to the film's exceeding quality.

As *DVD Drive-In* critic Douglas A. Waltz observes, "This is a fabulous film that manages to do what many of its bigger budget counterparts failed to do — deliver the goods both in story and the gore that Herschell was famous for."

There was a sometime-screenwriter in Chicago named Donald Stanford, who used the name "Dok." He wanted people to believe he was a doctor. He wasn't. He was just a guy who called himself Dok. He had written a script he called *The Secret of Dr. Alucard*. (Alucard is Dracula backwards.) There was a joke around the office that this thing was written by George Serutan, after Serutan, a medication used for constipation. (Serutan is Natures backward.) Dok Sanford kept saying this script was in demand, and that he had Sammy Davis Jr. and Frank Sinatra bidding for the rights to it. He said, "The problem is that I don't want to go out to California to mess with these guys." The reality was that he didn't have enough money to go to California Avenue, let alone to California. It was quite a transparent situation. It was as obvious a ploy as anyone has ever tried to pull in the movie business.

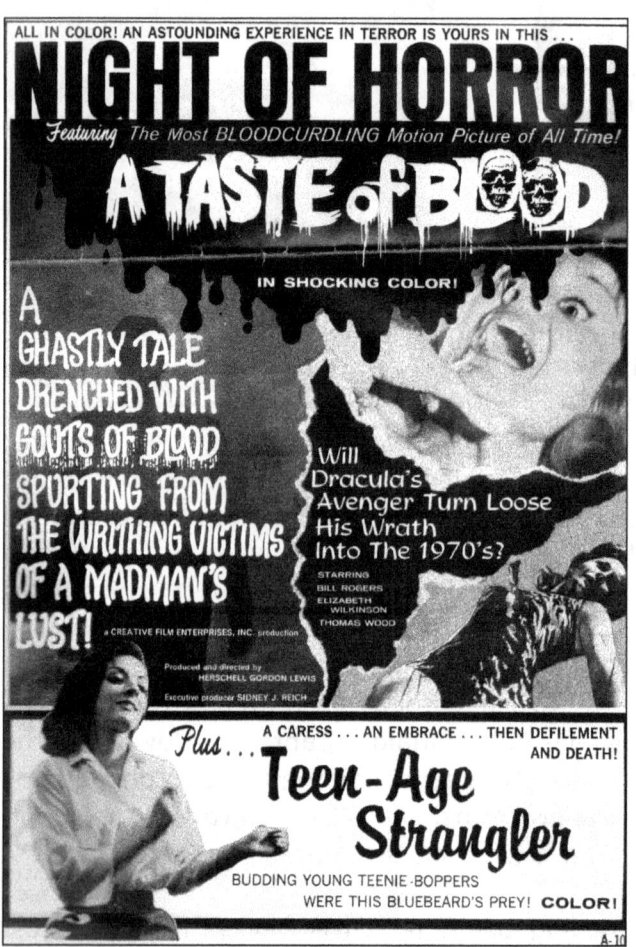

I made Dok Sanford a deal to buy his script. Length-wise, this thing was huge. I knew when I bought it that it would have to be trimmed dramatically in order to have a theater show it. I wasn't about to call it *The Secret of Dr. Alucard*, so I changed its title to *A Taste of Blood*.

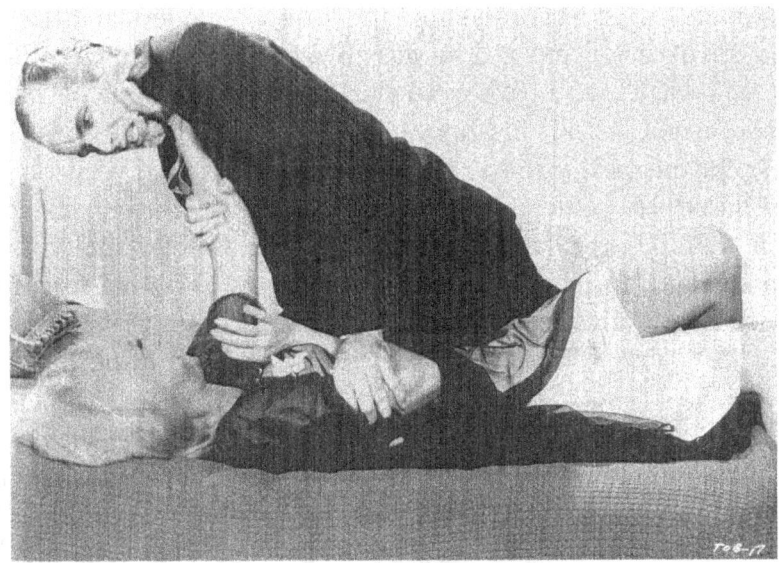
The vampire battles with a victim in the film *A Taste of Blood*.

Bill Rogers' character, it turns out, was a descendant of Count Dracula. He gets a bottle of Yugoslavian wine, which ends up containing the blood of Dracula. It then enters his bloodstream, and he begins to kill off the descendants of those who killed the original Dracula.

This movie had the longest shooting schedule I have ever had on a movie, which was fourteen days. We had to shoot some of it on the docks on Miami, and there's a scene in there of which I'm quite proud. We were somehow able to make a deal with a shipping line, and we had our casket lowered off the ship, the *Kinderdonc*, and it was a very nice and professional-looking effect. But there again, I knew I was going to have to get that in one take or lose that forever. Luckily for us, we got it in one take.

In an interesting side note, I had purchased the casket when I was working on the picture before this one. I told them, "You'll have to hold this casket until I get back to town." They couldn't understand what we were doing. They said, "Well, what about the deceased?" I said, "The deceased will wait." They didn't seem to have much of a sense of humor. Of course that's generic to our industry.

When we were shooting that scene while docked at the Port of Miami, another interesting thing happened. The longshoremen rule that area with an iron fist, and those words are carefully chosen, I assure you. We were told we could shoot from six to seven. I hired an actor with a Limey accent to play the sailor, and I made it very clear to him that he had to be on time because we only had that one hour to shoot the scene. "I understand that, I do," he said. So five o'clock came, and he was nowhere to be seen. Five-fifteen came, and he still wasn't there. We were starting to get nervous because no one had a phone number for this guy. So I said, "Just in case he doesn't show up, I'll dress for the part." We had a crew member who had very long hair, and I asked him to cut some of it off and give it to me. At five to six, it was very apparent that the man was not going to show up. So I became that character. I had a stocking cap that I pulled down over my ears, and I used the crew member's hair to give me something of a mustache.

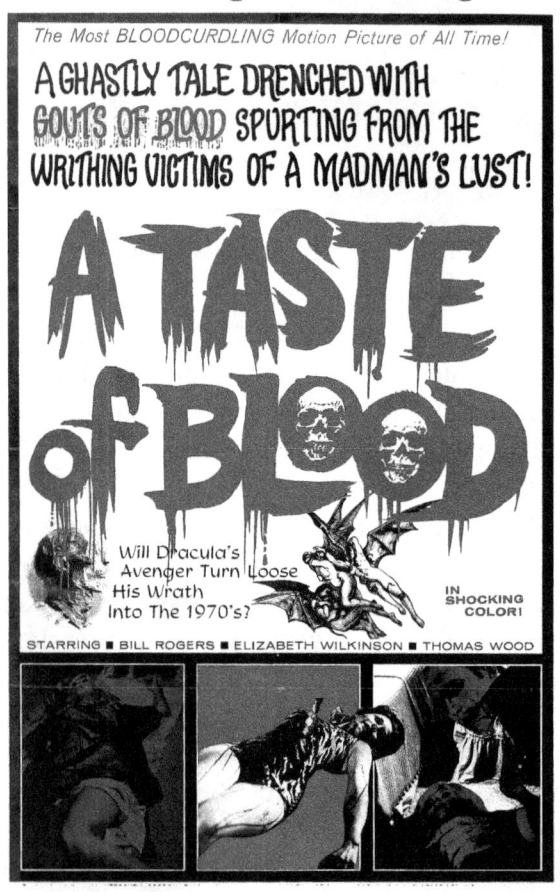

We got on the ship, and I kept stalling. Finally, one of the longshoremen said, "If you guys ain't finished by seven o'clock, we're going to throw your equipment into the bay!" So I said, "Okay, that solves the problem." So I became that character, assuming no one would ever guess who the character was. First, I had that cap pulled way down. Second, I was talking in that ridiculous limey accent. It was overdone, but it worked because the film was primarily for a U.S. audience, and a U.S. audience doesn't care if a British accent is overdone. I was not going to be doing something from *The King and I* here. But I took the part because there was no one else to do it.

Later, when we were mixing the film, that scene came on, and the editor said, "What are you doing in this film?" Well, my cover was blown, but that was strictly internal.

Ultimately, we had to intermix the day-for-night scenes with night-for-night. For day-for-night we had a polarizing filter that went over the lens of the camera, which turned the scene dark but didn't destroy the image. Well, some video technician saw the day-for-night shots and thought it was dark by accident. So he "fixed" it. Now, as a result, there's this mixture of scenes in which it's dark and then it's daylight and then it's dark and then it's daylight again. It doesn't work at all. I said to the film's distributor, Mike Vraney, when the videocassette first came out, "Hasn't anyone complained about that?" And he said, "Only you." As far as I know, to this day, that scene at the tail-end of the film with the Dracula character and his wife, still has those effects problems.

I screened this film for Roger Corman, who wanted to see some output. Roger and I were going to make a deal regarding a film called *Jackson County Jail*, but we never did. This was because his proposition made no business sense. I would have wound up financing the entire project in exchange for being a co-producer. That didn't make any sense to me at all.

A Taste of Blood played very well and the videocassettes and DVDs continue to sell, despite their having the day-for-night issues.

In 1966, Lewis met Fred M. Sandy, and the two men joined forces to establish Mayflower Pictures, Inc. With Sandy as executive producer and Lewis as producer and director, the two men would collaborate on four films. *The Gruesome Twosome* would be one of them.

Shot in just six days, *The Gruesome Twosome* would have the shortest shooting schedule of any Lewis gore film since *Blood Feast*. The result of this effort would be a respectable shocker the duo could be proud of. "I thought it was a charming little picture," Lewis has said. "It's gore served up with a sense of humor."

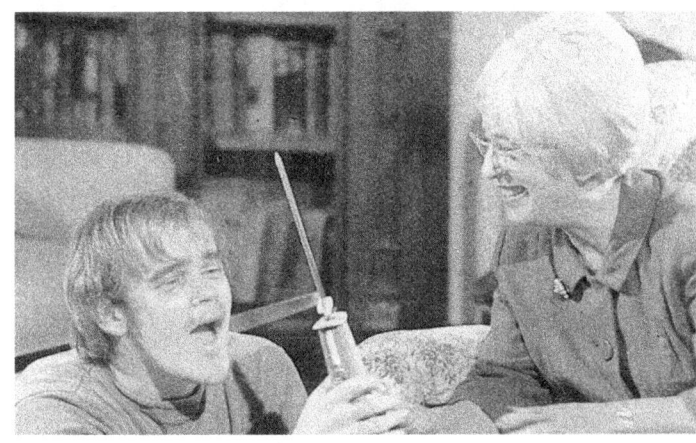

A scene from the Herschell Gordon Lewis film
The Gruesome Twosome.

The film, which claimed to feature "the most barbaric humor since the guillotine went out of style," would ultimately be one of a remarkable potpourri of six features released by Lewis in 1967.

The Gruesome Twosome had a problem I had not envisioned when I shot it, and that is the problem of appropriate running time. We had someone who had the responsibility of guessing the length. When you're shooting a movie where there's a combination of acting and dialogue, it's always a guess as to how much of the action one will hold. She guessed at one point that we already had over 70 minutes of running time. So by the time we were close to winding the thing down, I thought we were close to 80 minutes. Guess what, sports fans — she was way off the mark and we ended up with a little over 60 minutes of running time. Because of this, I had to stick a lot of footage back in there that I had planned to exclude from the finished film. And that still didn't make the movie long enough.

This problem of length was the genesis of the talking head routine, which we shot after I had gone back to Chicago. There was no reason to return to Florida to shoot this, because by this time the cast had scattered into the four winds. That opening sequence of *The Gruesome Twosome*, in which two wig blocks are having a discussion, occurred only because the running time was too short.

The main character of this film was a middle-aged woman, which was unusual for a movie of this type. Her name was Elizabeth Davis. She was a very fine actress who really took the role and ran with it at a pace I had not expected. She played a big role in making that movie what it was. One fascinating aspect of *The Gruesome Twosome* was that Elizabeth Davis had a pet cat, and we shot one scene with that cat. As we were filming, the cat was all over her lap, and ran away to the porch, and proved absolutely impossible to film. We then switched to

a stuffed animal. By this time we already had the first scene and we just figured, what the heck, with this being the kind of movie it was, it would make no difference. So anyone who likes to analyze movies to find mistakes — and my stuff is likely to keep them busy — will find that Mrs. Pringle's opening scene features a live cat, and from then on it's a stuffed cat. And you know what? In all these years, no one has ever pointed out that the cat — Napoleon was his name — changes from one scene to the next from being a live cat to being a stuffed one.

Chris Martell played Mrs. Pringle's idiot son, Rodney. And the plotline of *The Gruesome Twosome*, as is the case with all of my movies, was very primitive. She runs a wig shop, and Rodney scalps these young girls down in the basement in order to provide her with the makings of her wigs. The romantic lead was a girl named Gretchen Wells, and the key scene in the movie is when Rodney corners her in the basement. She then grabs something and stabs him in the eye. I had learned early on that eyeballs were just about as gruesome an effect as anyone could ever have. In fact, in my movies, there was only one crew member who was willing to squeeze an eyeball, and that was my son, Bob. He grew up with this business, and he had the job of eyeball squeezer. This was the first time we used this particular effect, and we made the mistake of getting a cow's eye for it. A cow's eye is the size of a football. It's unbelievably big, and it didn't look real even though it was. We wound up reshooting the scene with a fish eye. So in the end, the eye that Cathy pulls out of Rodney's head was a fish eye.

Our romantic male lead was a fellow named Rodney Bedell. He wasn't the greatest actor, but he was good on camera and he did whatever he was told. One day we were shooting a scene with Rodney that took place inside a car. At the end of shooting this scene in the car, I yelled "cut," which was a huge mistake. Rodney Bedell drove off in the car and there went every bit of our sound system with him! They'd all been wired. This was before wireless microphones. We had little wires running down people's pants and shirts. When he drove off, it just yanked the whole thing out of the sound recording machine! When you shoot a movie like that, you expect trouble. The problem is, the trouble you expect is never the trouble you get.

What's strange about *The Gruesome Twosome* is that after all the troubles we had, I never felt it justified the kind of business that movie has done from the word "go." Maybe it was the title, but that film has always done quite well. In some circles *The Gruesome Twosome* is regarded as the ultimate Herschell Gordon Lewis film. That fact puzzles me, but it also delights me. It just goes to show that for everyone who says something stinks, there is someone else to say, "This is excellent."

Alley Tramp – She-Devils on Wheels – Just for the Hell of It

"My only memory of the Alley Tramp *shoot was playing touch football with all of the male members of the cast and crew behind the motel where we were staying in Florida. The actual shooting of the film became almost incidental."*
—Herschell Gordon Lewis

Shot in a mere two days on 35mm, the sexploitation quickie *Alley Tramp* was crafted by Herschell Gordon Lewis from an outline by Allison Louise Downe and Paul Gordone. The film, shot in black-and-white for frequent Lewis collaborator Tom Dowd, would be one of the first films to tackle the issue of abortion.

The plot finds teenybopper Marie (Julie Ames) observing her parents having sex. She then contemplates losing her virginity and goes on an all-out mission to lose it. She practically attacks a distant cousin, Phil (Steve White of *Just for the Hell of It*), and the two of them end up having sex. Marie then becomes a full-fledged nymphomaniac, even going so far as to seduce her mother's lover. Marie soon becomes pregnant, and convinces cousin Phil to pay for an abortion.

The film has also been released under the alternate titles *I Am a Woman* and *Pleasure Me, Master*. Director Lewis is credited here with the pseudonym Armand Parys.

Alley Tramp was a Tom Dowd picture. I was simply the instrument through which that picture got shot. All of his movies took only two to four days to shoot. They all had the advantage of automatic distribution. Like most of Tom Dowd's films, *Alley Tramp* didn't have much of a plot. We gave Allison Louise Downe screenwriting credit, but it was actually Tom Dowd's script.

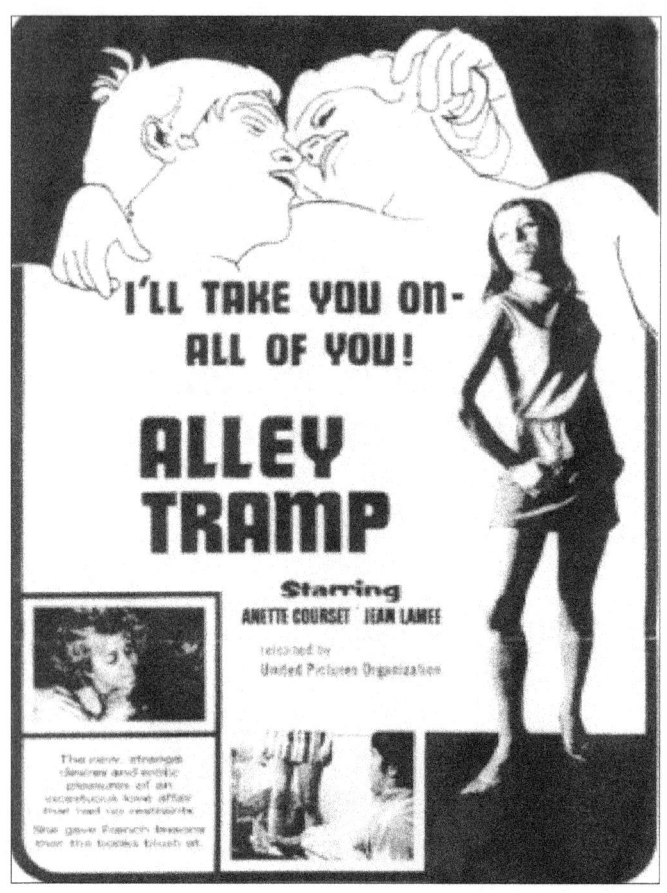

One aspect that Tom Dowd unintentionally superimposed on his output was that as long as it ran through the machine, and as long as there was a spicy scene or two, nothing else mattered. And as I remember this movie, I have the image that the lead got sick. She was only 16 or 17 years old, and she was seeing a much older man there from Hungary. There was a rumor that the man had infected her with a sexually transmitted disease. She would show up on set with a raging fever, and no one wanted to go near her.

But we did finish the picture.

Lewis and Fred Sandy decided to produce a female motorcycle picture as their next collaboration. "That came to mind because people within the industry were saying to me, 'You're always killing women. How about killing some men?' " This observation wasn't really true; as far back as *Two Thousand Maniacs!* Lewis had been an equal opportunity killer. But the idea of a female motorcycle gang appealed to Lewis and Sandy, and off they went to Miami to make the film, *She-Devils on Wheels*.

The film, which stars Betty Connell, Nancy Lee Noble, and Christie Wagner, follows a female motorcycle gang called The Maneaters. In between holding bike races and terrorizing locals, the gang wages war against an all-male rival gang.

"The combination of novelty and reality really pays off and forgives some of the dreadful scripting and melodramatic menopause involved," observes *DVD Verdict* critic Bill Gibron. "*She-Devils* is a demented delicacy where the girls just want to fight, frug, and fornicate as part of their fun."

My partner on *She-Devils on Wheels* was Fred Sandy. Fred was the father of Jerry Sandy, the American International Pictures distributor in Washington, D.C. Fred was an old-time exhibitor, who had retired to Columbia, South Carolina. He wanted to make movies to show his old friend, Sam Arkoff. Sam Arkoff, of course, ran American International, which was an independent movie company which envisioned itself as a hyper-competitor of companies like Metro-Goldwyn-Mayer, Paramount, and Fox. But really that was just Sam Arkoff's ego at work. He was quite a flashy character — a cigar-smoking type who was really generic to the movie business in those days. Fred wanted to make movies to show Sam Arkoff that he could make movies.

One of the movies Fred and I decided to make together was a female motorcycle picture. I had been seeing

a lot of motorcycle pictures, but they always focused on the men. They had women sitting on the backs of motorcycles, clinging for dear life to some husky fellow who was riding the Hog. That gave me the notion to make a movie about a female motorcycle gang.

We set up a little office in a hotel in Miami. We ran an ad looking for women who rode motorcycles. We didn't want stunt doubles, and we didn't want pretty girls. We wanted women who actually rode motorcycles, and it was quite clear in the advertising that we ran that we would settle for nothing less. And that's what we got. You can't imagine — well, maybe you can — some of the women who came out to audition for roles in *She-Devils on Wheels*.

We shot most of the chase scenes for the film at an abandoned airport called Amelia Earhart Field. I don't think it's still around today, but it was the perfect place to shoot because it had a long cement runway, and we could shoot whatever we wanted to shoot there. I would sometimes hang onto the back of a motorcycle and film while some of these women rode down the runway. It was quite an exhilarating experience.

Some of these gals were really quite strange. We had one girl who only had one front tooth — a great big tooth right in the middle of her mouth. Everyone called her Fang. One day — and it wasn't an important shooting day — she showed up late. I asked her what happened, and she said, "Oh, we had to bury my boyfriend. We had an accident on his bike, and I had to go to his funeral." It was just a throwaway line for her; it seemed of very little importance.

There was another woman named Agi Gyenes. She was of Hungarian extraction. Alex Ameripoor, our second unit cameraman, referred to her as "Agi the doggie." Well, one day, Agi had to prove that she could, in fact, ride a motorcycle. Where she got the one she used, I don't know. Everyone had to audition in that respect, because this was more important to me than being able to recite lines. She rode this bike in, and we were scattering. And Agi rode that motorcycle into the motel swimming pool! If she hadn't hit that pool, though, she might have hit a wall or something. It would have caused a much more dire consequence. But the motel, as you can imagine, was most displeased with us. There was oil all over the place. We hauled that thing out of the water, and nevertheless, we cast her in the movie. I felt there might be some exploitation value, although we never did make much of a point of it. That was a classic situation, and I wish we'd had a camera on when she did that.

Not only could Agi not ride a motorcycle, but she also could not recite lines. There was a line in that movie where Agi says, "No one pays attention to that senile old woman." Those words made no sense to her at all, and she kept ending it as a question. "No one pays attention to that senile old woman?" And you know, I never had more than two takes of anything. But I finally had to change the dialogue because she simply could not deliver that line correctly.

We shot *She-Devils on Wheels*, and I could see at once going in that we had a movie here that would be the first of my films since *Blood Feast* that would attract a wide enough distribution that we could open in multiple theaters.

Fred wanted to show off for Sam Arkoff. Because of this, the deal that we made for *She-Devils on Wheels* was an odd distribution arrangement. In about half the distribution areas, American International Pictures ran this picture together with one of theirs. It was a movie starring Tom Laughlin, titled *Born Losers*. This double feature ran on a supposed 50/50 split. In the other territories, we turned *She-Devils on Wheels* over to an independent distributor in that territory. For ex-

ample, in Chicago, which was where I was living at the time, there was an independent distributor named Jack Gilbreth, who handled all the distribution for Russ Meyer. He was used to working with exploitation pictures. As I recall, that was the biggest opening we ever had in one market; we had 32 prints, and we used every one of them for the Chicago opening. But the odd thing with *She-Devils on Wheels* and the relationship with Sam Arkoff and American International Pictures was that invariably, when we shared the limelight with their movie, we made less money than we did when we went on our own. I believe that might have cured Fred Sandy about the notion of competing financially with AIP. He still wanted to compete with them emotionally, but he understood a little better — especially as a former exhibitor — what the perils might be in entrusting a movie with a distributor whose goals were not necessarily to enhance the coffers of the producer. Incidentally, later on, Tom Laughlin, the star of *Born Losers*, sued American International Pictures.

I have never had any negative feelings regarding what happened with *She-Devils on Wheels*. We had a good time making it, and we certainly had a profitable time showing it.

Shot back to back with *She-Devils on Wheels*, *Just for the Hell of It* would be a minor Lewis film focusing on juvenile delinquency. Lewis has called the project a film he likes but "apparently no one else does," and has stated his belief that it should have been a cult film. *Just for the Hell of It* features a handful of Lewis regulars, including Ray Sager, Rodney Bedell, Agi Gyenes, Nancy Lee Noble, and Steve White, among others.

The film's storyline follows a teen gang led by Dexter (Sager). The gang terrorizes the residents of a small Florida town, harasses people, and mindlessly destroys anyone and everything that gets in their way.

"For those of you with a penchant for vintage exploitation, you can do a lot worse than *Just for the Hell of It*," writes *Girls, Guns, and Ghouls* critic Boris Lugosi. "Aside from any thematic concerns, you've got the great sixties decor, clothes and soundtrack. After these surface thrills you can appreciate the pretty confronting violence and themes. Lewis has crafted a fairly potent essay on mindless evil, despite the sometimes clunky performances and low budget."

Just for the Hell of It was about a bunch of wild kids. What we wanted to show was what was becoming a headline element at that time — kids running wild and doing whatever they felt like doing. That was the idea behind that film. It was a morality play. But it's a morality play mixed with my personal philosophy of filmmaking, which is get some bodies in the seats.

One thing that might interest you is that I briefly considered casting Veronica Lake in the film. Bill Kerwin was living in a house in Miami with Veronica Lake. She wasn't a lover, but she also lived in that house. Veronica

Lake had a very peculiar motion picture history. She never was regarded as a talent of any sort. Her main claim to fame was a hairdo in which her hair hung over one eye. That's how she was remembered. And she had appeared in one picture with Fredric March, who had to be as fine an actor as any who had ever appeared on screen. The story was that he didn't want the movie released because of Veronica Lake, but that may just be folklore.

By the time we ran across her, she was long in the tooth and had no value whatever. Bill Kerwin said, "Put her in this movie." We had no reason to. There was nothing there. But there was another problem, as well, and that was that Veronica Lake was a member of the Screen Actors Guild. Usually when I worked with actors like Bill Kerwin, who was a member of the Guild, they would work under a pseudonym because they wanted to be in a picture. But not Veronica Lake. I could see that putting her in a picture — even though there was a certain amount of name value — would be more liability than asset. So my entire association with Veronica Lake was my saying hello and the two of us exchanging pleasantries. That's as far as it went.

Just for the Hell of It was a minor picture of mine. It wasn't enough of an effort for me to have many memories of it.

The Psychic – How to Make a Doll – The Ecstasies of Women

"With a film like The Ecstasies of Women — *a film with no rehearsal time and no one with any acting talent — you have to have a primitive plotline, and this film did not disappoint."*
—Herschell Gordon Lewis

Soon James Hurley was back to his old tricks. Having already walked away from *Something Weird* after Lewis had transformed it into something more commercial, Hurley sought to make a second movie about extra-sensory perception. And once again, this film, The Psychic, would be a sort of tribute to his hero Peter Hurkos. Hurley again approached Lewis, this time wanting him to work on the film only in the capacity of cinematographer. The plan was that Hurley would double as both screenwriter and director. However, this arrangement soon fell apart when it became apparent that Hurley had no notion of how to direct a film.

When the film was released, it did less business than Hurley and his financier (good old Stan Kohlberg) had anticipated. Kohlberg, who constantly pronounced the opinion that the word "Copenhagen" in a film title would guarantee success, then conceived the idea to integrate softcore adult footage into the film and re-title it with the nonsensical moniker *Copenhagen's Psychic Lovers*.

"Needless to say, the result is an awkward mess," writes *Movie Musings and Grumblings* critic Dave Sindelar, "but, like Ed Wood's *Glen or Glenda*, you can see something more substantial trying to glimmer through. Still, the oddest thing I found about the movie is that the child actors are fairly good, which I found rather strange, since [Hurley] seemed unable to coax decent performances from the adults. This one is definitely an oddity."

Once again, film historians have repeatedly listed *The Psychic* as being a Herschell Gordon Lewis picture. Because of this, Lewis has agreed to set the record straight in this volume.

As you'll remember, James Hurley was the man behind the film *Something Weird*. When that film didn't turn out as he had hoped it would, he decided to make his own film. That film would be called *The Psychic*. It was the same kind of film, and again it was a tribute to Peter Hurkos, the resident would-be psychic. I was hired as cameraman this time out, and that was it. But obviously it was impossible to be only the cameraman. In order to get something on film, there has to be something going on in front of the camera.

What happened with *The Psychic* was really funny. James Hurley was going to distribute this movie himself, and he made a bit of a deal with the devil by making a deal with Stan Kohlberg. Kohlberg was, you'll remember, the "partner" Dave Friedman, Sid Reich, and I had sued over the income from *Two Thousand Maniacs!* and *Color Me Blood Red*. I don't know if his hero Peter Hurkos advised him to do this, and if he did, there was absolutely no reason to have any reliance on

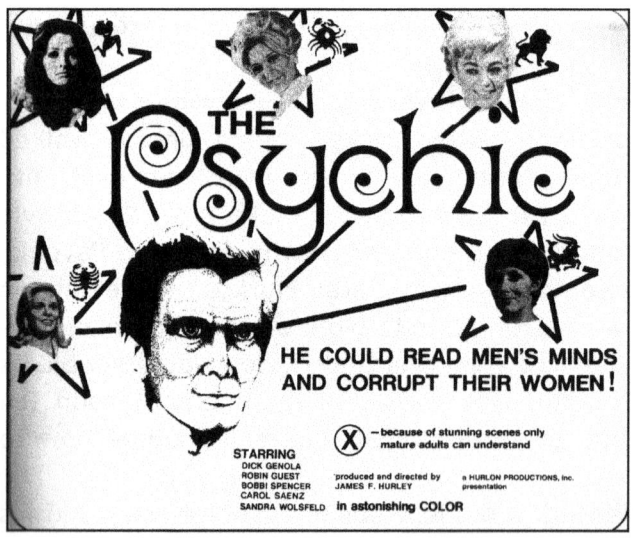

Peter Hurkos' capabilities. Kohlberg, who felt he knew all the answers to everything, retitled the movie. Kohlberg felt, just as James Hurley believed that nothing could be awry if it had to do with extra-sensory perception, and that nothing could go wrong if its title contained the word "Copenhagen." So

Kohlberg rechristened the film as *Copenhagen's Psychic Lovers*, which I believe is just a scream for a title. There's nothing about that title that suggests anything that happens in that film, as it has absolutely nothing to do with Copenhagen.

James Hurley once again wrote the screenplay for *The Psychic*. As with *Something Weird*, the lead character in *The Psychic* gets injured when he gets hit with an electrical wire. This time he gets extra-sensory capabilities, and they gradually wear off. The plotline does make a little sense in that respect, but then the character goes to New York and touts himself as a psychic. He begins predicting what's going to happen and solving crimes and problems. Gradually, because he's losing his powers, he becomes a joke.

That film is still around today. The thing that bothers me about it is that every now and then I'll see something about the film where they'll list me as the originator! That, I assure you, was not the case. I was strictly the cameraman on *The Psychic*.

When David Chudnow came to Lewis with a script his wife had written called *How to Make a Doll*, Lewis knew at once the project was awful. But the upsides outweighed the down; Chudnow was putting up the money for the picture, and here was yet another chance to leave windy Chicago for the warmer climate of Florida.

"The movie was pretty awful," Lewis would later concede. "It was a comedy that lacked one important element, and that was humor." Lewis believed *How to Make a Doll* could possibly have been a better film if he'd had a bigger budget to work with. With no money to use for special effects, Lewis had relied heavily on smoke bombs to make it appear as though the girls were appearing in a puff of smoke. In hindsight, Lewis believes this was the type of picture that should have been left to the Blake Edwardses of the world.

David Chudnow, a film veteran from Beverly Hills, made his money scoring movies for a company called Pine-Thomas, which was a respected independent production company. His son, Byron Chudnow, was a film editor at Twentieth-Century Fox. Dave Chudnow saw a movie I made called *Moonshine Mountain.* He told me on the phone before we actually met, "You're my kind of guy. Let's get together and make a movie." My attitude was then as it is now — you want to put up the money, buddy, you got yourself a deal. And he did.

It turned out that his wife, Rosamond, had written a script. It was titled *How to Make a Doll.* It was supposed to be a comedy. We weren't really geared for comedy. But Dave Chudnow told me he would have no problem distributing this picture no matter what genre it fell into. What we were really going to do was get his wife some recognition. She had been living in the shadow of Dave Chudnow, who wasn't really on the A-list — maybe the B-list — and she felt this would be her chance to shine. The script was, I thought, a very thin comedy.

We shot it in Miami. Dave did get some distribution on it, and it played around some. I never would have made the movie if Dave Chudnow had not been behind it.

Later on, Dave and his son Byron made a movie called *The Incredible Dobermans.* According to Dave's son, the film did quite well. My response was, well then how come our picture didn't do that well? But I had no complaints. I had no investment whatever in *How to Make a Doll*, and it was a no-brainer to make it. It was no work, and no effects were needed.

How to Make a Doll is certainly not a footnote to motion picture history. It barely belongs in any kind of listing, except that yeah, I did make it.

Lewis collaborated with Tom Dowd once again on another nudie picture, *The Ecstasies of Women*. The concept behind the film was Dowd's, and Lewis again delivered a made-to-order film for the exhibitor. The film's plot was rather thin, focusing on a man who remembers his many loves during his bachelor party. In short, it was an excuse to show dancing women in various states of undress.

The film starred Walter Camp, Bonnie Clark, and Dowd discovery Sharon Matt, who would later appear in the Lewis and Dowd collaboration *Linda and Abilene*. Like all Tom Dowd pictures, *The Ecstasies of Women* made a healthy profit.

This was another Tom Dowd "classic," which will explain why it's lost today. As you will recall, Tom had ordered his son, Kevin, to destroy all of his films. As Tom's "staff director," I directed all his films, whether he shot them in Chicago or in California. This particular film was shot in California.

The film was about a bachelor party being thrown for someone who is getting married. Reminiscing, this character goes back over all of the many women he has bedded in his lifetime.

Tom Dowd had a discovery named Sharon Matt, and in the film she played a character named Philomena. Sharon's primary asset was that she looked like the most innocent and childlike creature

113

you could ever find. She had a smile that could melt an iceberg. She appeared in a couple of Tom's movies, and ultimately her husband, Dennis, a commercial artist, wound up coming to Chicago to work in the art department at my advertising agency. He had delusions about himself. One of his terms when he agreed to come to work for me in Chicago was that we would hold a one-man art show to display his work. In a moment of insanity, I agreed to that. Then when it came time to have the show, he didn't have enough art to carry the display. We then hired models to pose in the gallery so the people who came would have something to look at.

I don't really recall much about the shooting of *The Ecstasies of Women*. I don't really consider it one of my films — it's Tom Dowd's. I was just along for the ride. But as I have said many times, Tom Dowd never made a loser. Looking back over the cast, I can't tell you much about them because almost everyone involved used a pseudonym on the film.

Linda and Abilene – The Wizard of Gore – Miss Nymphet's Zap-In

> *"Our film,* Linda and Abilene, *was a western of sorts. However, there were telephone wires hanging all around the saloon area, making it difficult to shoot without getting them in the frame. Tom Dowd didn't care at all. He said, 'Just go ahead and film it with the wires in the shot.' And he was probably right. Nobody who showed these movies or went to them cared about such things."*
>
> —Herschell Gordon Lewis

Tom Dowd's next idea was a sexploitation western about lesbian cowgirls. Lewis agreed to direct the picture, Linda and Abilene, and headed off with Tom to California to shoot it. Interestingly, the ranch where the film was shot was also (unbeknownst to Lewis and crew) the home of Charles Manson and his murderous cult. The Spahn Ranch was also home to a broken-down stuntman, a blind rancher, and anachronistic telephone lines that got in the way of numerous shots.

"It was a strange place to shoot a movie," Lewis would later say. "But the price was right." In the low-budget filmmaking world of Herschell Gordon Lewis, little else mattered. And that thrifty attitude paid off; like all Tom Dowd films, Linda and Abilene made a small fortune at the box office.

We shot *Linda and Abilene* at the Spahn Ranch in California. Unbeknownst to us at the time, the infamous serial killer Charles Manson and his gang lived there. This was just before they went on their murderous rampage. We would see these people just hanging around, and I knew something was awry. They acted very peculiarly. For example, they had a dog, and they put a bell around the dog's neck. Every time the dog moved, the bell would sound and it would drive him absolutely crazy. So one of the people working on the crew went to take the bell off and was told, "If you wanna live to see sundown, you leave that alone!"

We shot *Linda and Abilene* there at the ranch, with Sharon Matt once again. She was the female lead in this picture, again playing the ingénue. The plotline was a rather simplistic one. It was about a boy and girl — sibling orphans — who suddenly realize that they have a strong sensual attraction for one another. This drives the boy away to this ranch, where he meets another girl and starts fooling around with her. Then another man begins to come after Sharon Matt. And that was the entire plot.

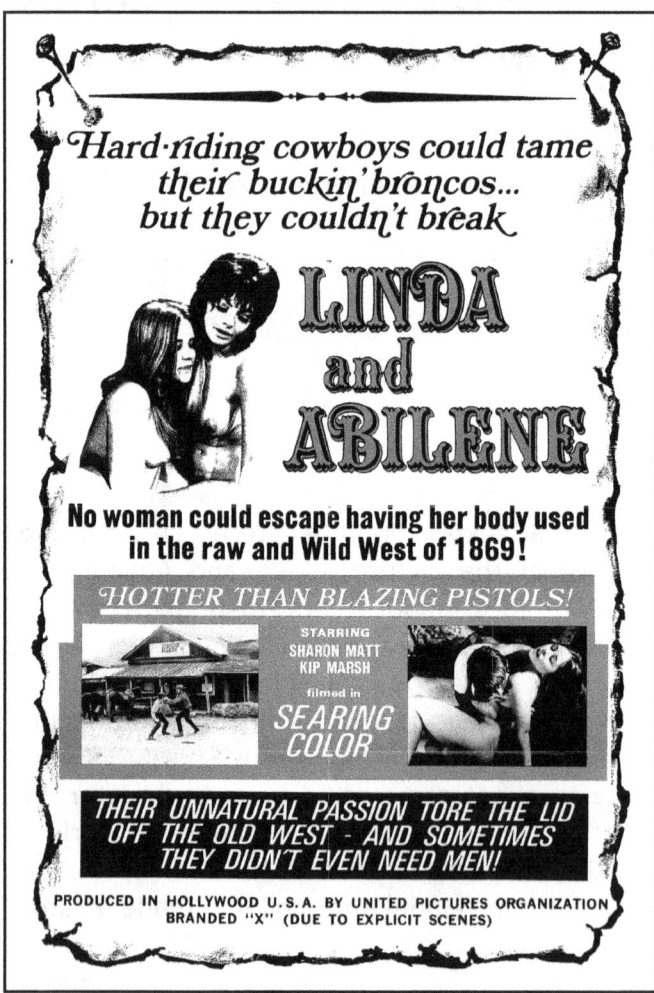

Allison Louise Downe was once again credited with writing the screenplay, but we gave her credit for a lot of scripts. The truth is that the scripts for every Tom Dowd film were made up on the fly. The actors would say, "What do I say here?" And Allison Louise Downe contributed to those lines of dialogue as much as anyone else.

Bethel "Buck" Buckalew was my production manager on this film. Today Buck is probably best known as the director of films like *Southern Comfort*, *Tobacco Rooty*, and *Sassy Sue*. He was one of the best production managers I have ever met in my life. In a matter of hours he could build a set that would have taken anyone else days to put together. He was my production manager on a number of films. We were in the middle of shooting this film, and I came down with the flu. I could barely move or breathe. I just felt terrible. Buck Buckalew gave me a shot of something, and I was back on my feet in four to six hours. I said, "You ought to patent that stuff." And he said, "You don't even want to know what it is." I suspected it was some sort of antibiotic, but who knows?

As I remember it, the advertising campaign was fairly strong. We played up the western aspect of the film, with a very sexual overtone. There was a newspaper called *The National Insider*. The editor of that publication suggested that we hold a contest in which the winner got to appear in the film, so we did. A girl won the contest, and she got to appear in two Tom Dowd films. We built some publicity out of that.

This was a typical Tom Dowd movie, and there were almost no outtakes at all. Again, this wasn't a film that originated with me; I was simply the director and the cameraman working at Tom's behest.

Things get hot and heavy in this scene from Lewis's sexploitation western *Linda and Abilene*.

With *The Wizard of Gore*, Lewis returned to the genre he created back in 1963 — the gore film. *The Wizard of Gore*, another collaboration with Fred Sandy, followed a talk show hostess and her boyfriend attempting to uncover the secrets of a suspicious magician with the ability to control people's thoughts.

"Herschell Gordon Lewis must have slipped everything into maximum overdrive," writes *A Taste of Blood* author Christopher Wayne Curry, "for it took 15 years for many to realize the overt reverence of this film. Lewis laid waste to circumventing taboos. He made no excuses and pulled no punches. The film is an unadulterated, premeditated exercise in bloodletting. (Even by today's standards, it is still effectively repellent.) In short, it was the ultimate gorefest."

Montag the Magician (Ray Sager) works his bloody magic in this scene from *The Wizard of Gore*.

The Wizard of Gore was another peculiar picture. We shot that one in Chicago. In subsequent years, this picture has grown in stature, which I've never felt it deserved. This, to me, was always just a minor effort. But there are those who say it is a superior film because they call it "gore mixed with Zen," which I find humorous.

Fred Sandy was my partner on that picture. Fred was an old film business veteran, and he wanted desperately to get back into the film business. Together we formed a company called Mayflower Pictures, and one of the films this company was going to make was *The Wizard of Gore*. Fred was the executive producer, and I was the producer and director. The difference is that a producer actually does something. My definition of an executive producer is a schmuck with a checkbook.

The screenplay was credited to Alan Kahn. Alan was a young copywriter in my advertising office. He was constantly exposed to what we were doing, and he provided me with the bare bones of this story. I didn't pay much attention to plotline here, because I knew we were going to pretty much wing it as we shot it. But we gave him the credit. We often did that — gave people screen credits — but what Alan did here wasn't so much screenwriting as it was making an outline. If you look at the DVD of *Wizard of Gore* (which I'm amazed still exists and they're still selling them), it'll say "special technical effects by Sheldon Seymour," which was of course me.

The male lead in the picture was a guy named Wayne Ratay, who worked for IBM. He called on me to try to sell me an IBM composer, and I wound up casting him as the lead in this film. The female lead was a woman named Judy Cler, who was a Chicago model with aspirations of becoming an actress. She was actually pretty good, as I recall.

It was a good-natured shoot all the way through with only one exception. Ray Sager was part of our filmmaking gang, and he was going to be on the crew of this movie. The first scene we shot was in a high-rise building on Lakeshore Drive. Fred Sandy had become convinced that he was an integral part of production. So he started directing the actor cast as Montag the Magician. They got into a huge argument, and the guy said, "For what you guys are paying me, I don't need this crap!" And he walked out. We were in the lobby of this big building, and the actor stood outside the front door waiting for someone to bring him back inside so Fred could apologize, which was never going to happen. I didn't know what to do. Fred was wrong, but he was my partner. So, as he was standing out there, Ray Sager was looking for something to do. I said, "Ray, do you want to be Montag the Magician?" And Ray said, "Why not?" And just that spontaneously, Ray Sager became Montag the Magician.

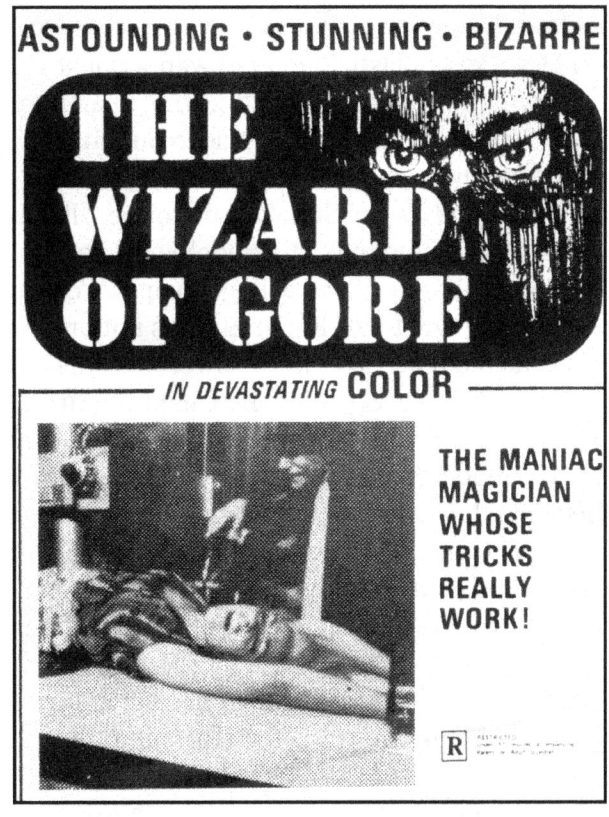

I had an Aunt Jane. Everyone has an Aunt Jane. Well, my Aunt Jane was very impressed that I was making movies. She didn't know anything about them, but she was impressed. So I received a phone call from Aunt Jane. She said, "Your cousin, Roger Strauss, wants to work with you." I didn't even know I had a cousin named Roger Strauss! I said, "If he's willing to work on the crew for minimum wage, Roger Strauss can work on my new movie, *The Wizard of Gore*." In came Roger Strauss, a younger relative, and he became a part of the crew.

Whenever we shot at an apartment building or in someone's home, I did the electrical hook-up myself. The reason I did was because the only thing we had to fear was blowing out someone's television set or having the whole house go dark, which will happen if you plug a bunch of lights into a single outlet. Our lights were 240 volts, and we had a stepdown to 120. We also had the reverse, where we could push 120 up to 240, which is what we were using in this instance. We found a power box on the same floor of this apartment building where we were going to be shooting.

This is where I was going to shoot what I referred to as my "ultimate effect." In this scene, Montag the Magician would literally rip a body to pieces. We bought a goat carcass for that purpose, and Judy Cler was going to have herself ripped to pieces. We went to K-Mart and bought a shag rug and a sheet of plastic. I did not want to destroy somebody's beautiful Persian rug, which is what they had in this apartment. We stuck a sheet of plastic over their rug, and then we placed our shag carpet over that. This was where this total dismemberment was going to take place. I was trying to set this thing up, and Roger Strauss said to me, "I've seen you make these electrical hook-ups. Let me make this hook-up. I know just how to do it." Like a moron I said, "That would be a huge help." We started setting up and suddenly everything went out. Roger Strauss not only blew out the power box, but he also started a fire in it! This power box was outside the apartment, down the hall somewhere. So someone called the fire department, and they threw us out of there! And here was our goat carcass and our rug from K-Mart, sitting on the floor of this apartment. I could not argue with them — not only because they were so angry, but also because they were threatening to call the police and seize our equipment. I said, "It's time to get out," and off we went. And that destroyed my ultimate effect. I could not get another goat carcass within the framework of what we had to work with.

If you look at that scene in *The Wizard of Gore*, you'll see that the entire scene was changed. Instead of her being torn to shreds, something different happens. As he's ripping the stuff out of her, she begins to laugh and sits up and the entire ending of the picture changes. So this combination of gore and zen was accidental, and I should give Roger Strauss credit for that.

Taking a cue from the popular television series *Rowan and Martin's Laugh-In*, Lewis and his partner Fred Sandy conceived a comedic sex-ploitation picture comprised of short vignettes. They titled it *Miss Nymphet's Zap-In*. The film featured Dixie Donovan, Tony Mark, and Luanne Roberts. In an ingenious move to draw more attention to the film, Lewis gave *Miss Nymphet* a self-imposed "X" rating. Of course he knew that the film was an "R" at worst, but he also knew the "X" would make the film appear to be more risqué than it actually was.

The film performed well at the box office, and later got a second run as the TV series it was inspired by experienced a backlash and eventually got cancelled. "I couldn't keep enough prints in circulation," Lewis recalls. "It played its heart out."

My partner on *Miss Nymphet's Zap-In* was Fred Sandy, and we made it for our Mayflower Pictures company. At the time there was a popular TV show called *Rowan and Martin's Laugh-In*, which was where Goldie Hawn made her first appearances. We decided to make a sexy version of that show, and thus *Miss Nymphet's Zap-In* was born. The film ultimately did quite well because it was made with high good humor. And this was at a time when films of its type were so deadly serious. So our film was sort of a refreshing change because nobody took it too seriously.

Miss Nymphet's Zap-In was a series of comedic episodes. Each episode lasted anywhere from thirty seconds to three minutes. Then, between the sequences, we had the entire cast tap dancing. They would then

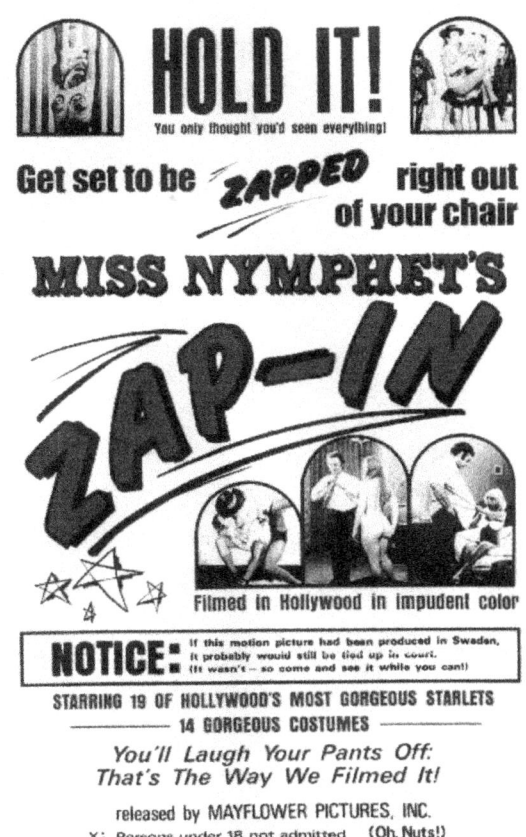

stop at the count of three and yell at the camera, "Zap!" That was the transition between scenes. Everyone in the film had at least two roles, and sometimes as many as three or four. Each of the episodes was short, so if someone hated one, another episode came on before he could say, "I hated that." That worked out very well. We had a lot of people in that movie, but many of them worked only one day. It became possible because each episode stood alone.

I remember giving Buck Buckalew a role in that film. There was a sequence in which a cannibal girl ate a missionary. Buck played the missionary. She said something like, "I'm going to have my dinner in bed," or something like that. And we stuck Buck Buckalew into a stew pot. He was always a very cooperative type of person, which is important when you're making these kinds of low-budget films.

One thing I did on that movie that really had me scared at the time was put supers on some of the scenes. I wound the film backwards, and then shot a white title against a stark black background. It was scary because if it didn't work, it would completely destroy that scene. Luckily, it did work. But it very easily could not have. You have to make sure when you wind the film back that the sprocket holes hit in exactly the same place they did before. If they don't, that super could run off the screen.

I gave the film a self-imposed "X" rating. There was no point submitting it to the Motion Picture Association of America. Eventually we paired that film with another movie I directed but owned no part of called *Black Love*.

Black Love – This Stuff'll Kill Ya! – Year of the Yahoo!

"One of the crosses I had to bear on This Stuff'll Kill Ya! *was the lack of availability for what you might call acting talent. Talent was lean, but enthusiasm was rather high."*

—Herschell Gordon Lewis

In 1971 the films *Sweet Sweetback's Baadasssss Song* and *Shaft* began a new trend in cinema known as "blaxploitation." These were films — some of which were directed by white directors — that featured primarily black casts. By 1972, major and independent studios alike were cranking out films with predominantly black casts. And these films were making money. Naturally, filmmakers who were already working in the exploitation field soon tried their hands at making such films. Lewis would be no exception.

Lewis was approached by a businessman named Bob Smith, who was interested in making a hybrid film that contained all the elements of a sexploitation picture but with an all-black cast. Lewis agreed to make the film, which would be titled *Black Love.*

Today the film is lost and very little information on it survives.

Black Love was owned and conceived by a black businessman named Bob Smith, who owned some Baskin & Robbins outlets in Chicago. He was very serious about making a serious sex movie. He wanted to make a sexy film with black actors in it. So I just directed that movie and was the cameraman, as usual.

We shot the film in three days. *Black Love* was shot entirely inside people's apartments. It was more dedicated to close-ups than any movie I can recall ever being involved with. The direction and the cinematography of that movie were a snap.

I had absolutely nothing to do with the talent. Bob Smith had connections to cast that movie, and I asked no questions. I remember one of the guys he cast had a huge hole in his shoulder. It looked very strange on camera, so we stuffed it with mortician's wax and then added color to it. I felt we had made a huge step forward in motion picture make-up.

There is one sequence in *Black Love* in which a little girl — she had to be seven or eight years old — stumbles into a room and catches her parents making the beast with two backs. She says, "Oh my goodness," and she stares in astonishment. As you might imagine, those two pieces of the scene were shot separately, a long time apart. The little girl had no idea what she was supposed to be looking at.

When Bob Smith turned the movie over to Stan Kohlberg for distribution, it was decided that it would be paired up with *Miss*

Nymphet's Zap-In. *Miss Nymphet* had already played around a bit by this time. I was not thrilled to be working with Kohlberg again because this was at a time when he and I were completely on the outs. I believe it was after I had settled my lawsuit against him.

I was pleased with the advertising campaign I conceived. "Is there a difference? See for yourself in *Black Love*."

Black Love played for a long time. All I know is what Bob Smith told me. He said he had to keep making prints because the picture was playing and playing and playing. The picture had a big playoff, and as far as I know it is the only black picture of its kind ever made.

Lewis' next picture, *This Stuff'll Kill Ya!*, would be a sort of hybrid of *Moonshine Mountain* and *Two Thousand Maniacs!*, with a little country/western music thrown in for good measure. The film's storyline included moonshine, a redneck con man, and federal agents, along with a small helping of gore. The film, shot in Oklahoma, was also chock full of new country tunes, all of which were penned by Lewis himself.

While *This Stuff'll Kill Ya!* is a minor Lewis effort by any standard, it is significant because it featured the return of *The Treasure of the Sierra Madre* star Tim Holt and marked the debut of future *Dr. Giggles* star Larry Drake.

I shot *This Stuff'll Kill Ya!* in Oklahoma City. Way back in the annals of history I had been a producer and director at the television station WKY in Oklahoma City. WKY was, and is, owned by *The Daily Oklahoman*, which is the big newspaper in Oklahoma. To this day, I have seen very few television stations that were as well-appointed as WKY. I ultimately left there when I went back into the advertising business. But I still had connections there. One of the programs I directed when I was there was called *The Chuckwagon Boys.*

There were three Chuckwagon Boys — two guitars and a string bass. One of the Chuckwagon Boys was a fellow named Jack Beasley. Years later I learned that Jack Beasley had purchased a radio station in Oklahoma that he called KJAC. KJAC had a studio, and we were talking about shooting this movie in Oklahoma City because I still knew some people there. I was in touch with Jack Beasley, and he said, "Shoot it in my studio." This was a

radio studio, but it was big and it was soundproof. This made complete sense to me, and that's why we made that movie in Oklahoma City. Jack Beasley gave us a truck to drive and made his studio completely available to us.

On my crew I had an Iranian named Alex Ameripoor. He was convinced that the finest movie anyone had ever made anywhere and at any time was a movie called *The Treasure of the Sierra Madre.* That film starred Walter Huston, Humphrey Bogart, and a then-young actor named Tim Holt. By this time, both Humphrey Bogart and Walter Huston were dead, and I knew nothing of Tim Holt. Well, when I got to Oklahoma City, whom did I discover there selling time for the radio? Tim Holt. I couldn't believe it. Here was a guy who was a legitimate actor! So he had to be in this movie, and he agreed to appear in it. He hadn't been in a movie in years and years, and this looked like a kick for him. Alex Ameripoor was in absolute ecstasy. Alex carried a 16mm print of *The Treasure of the Sierra Madre* with him everywhere he went, and would screen it for anyone at any time. I'm sure he had watched that film by himself at least 100 times. He just had a fanatical love for that movie. Tim Holt, by this time, was just a shell of what he had once been; he was not only long in the tooth, but also black in the tooth. He was considerably older than the Tim Holt of *The Treasure of the Sierra Madre.* In fact, I asked Alex if he had met Tim Holt yet, and Alex said sadly, "I met the wreckage of Tim Holt."

Even at that point, having not acted in many years, Tim Holt could have given anyone in that cast acting lessons. He was still a consummate actor. He didn't have a very big role in the film, but it was a pleasure to have him there.

We had a young actor on that film named Larry Drake, who was a student at the University of Oklahoma. He would later become famous as the half-wit on the television show *L.A. Law*. Again, quite the good and accomplished young actor, but not the leading man type.

In the end, *This Stuff'll Kill Ya!* did not do all that well at the box office. It was sort of an interlude, but at least I can say I made a movie with Tim Holt.

Year of the Yahoo! is an interesting entry in the Herschell Gordon Lewis filmography. "The title comes from Jonathan Swift's *Gulliver's Travels*," Lewis explains. The film, a sort of precursor to the Robin Williams vehicle *Man of the Year*, tells the tale of a famous country/western singer who runs for the U.S. Senate. *Year of the Yahoo!* features then-popular musician Claude King, who sings a number of songs once again written by Lewis himself.

"*Year of the Yahoo!* was a dud," Lewis would later say. It underperformed at the box office despite its playing in many theaters that would not usually show a Herschell Gordon Lewis film. Lewis believes the film's lack of success may have been partly due to the untimely release of the similarly themed Robert Redford vehicle, *The Candidate*.

We were originally going to have Roger Miller, the singer and songwriter known for songs like "Dang Me" and "King of the Road," as our lead in *Year of the Yahoo!* I was warned by a number of people that he had some personal problems and would disappear for days on end. That was all we needed to slow down production, so I decided instead to cast a country/western artist named Claude King. Claude was a very respectable country/western artist. He had one hit record, "Wolverton Mountain," back in 1962. With all due respect to Claude King, I never could understand why that song was a hit; something about it just didn't scan for me.

Year of the Yahoo! was about a country/Western singer who runs for the U.S. Senate. It was a sort of satire. There is nothing in that movie that has anything to do with the gore that I am usually associated with. I had begun to feel that my days were numbered in that particular area, which is one reason why I made this film.

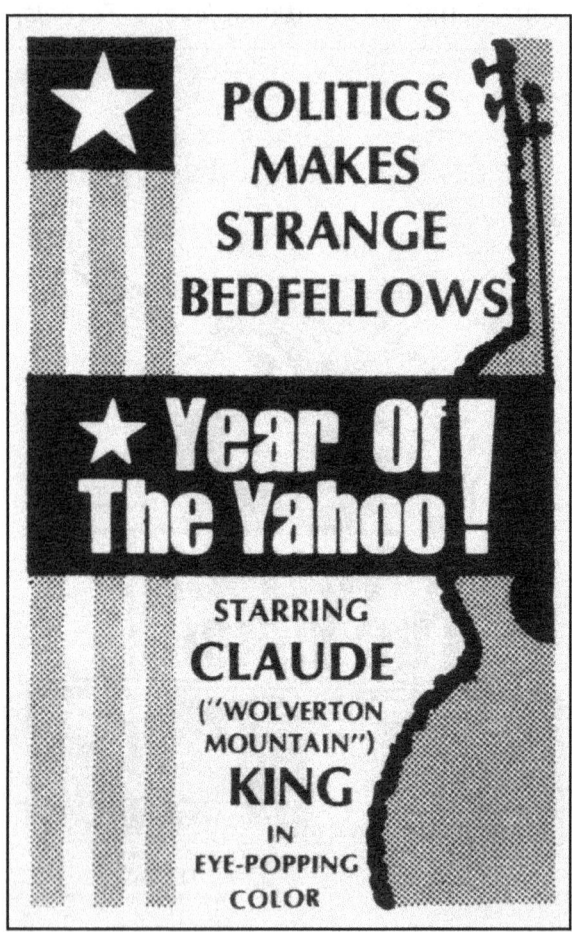

Ray Sager was also in the film, and the female lead was a girl named Ronna Riddle. And of course we had Taalkius Blank, using the name Jeffrey Allen, as the old-time politician in the movie. This was, in many ways, just my usual gang, along with Claude King and his band.

What happened with *Year of the Yahoo!* was peculiar. It played in theaters that would never have touched any of my other movies. In that respect, you could say it widened the field. But the result of it was not the same; they didn't play another of my pictures to accompany it. It simply stood alone as a very minor monolith in a rather odd progression. It made a little bit of money, but nothing like I had become accustomed to with the gore movies.

The Gore Gore Girls – Blood Feast 2: All U Can Eat – The Uh! Oh! Show

"I found myself infected once again. I've often maintained that making movies is like having malaria; you think you're over it, but it lurks in the bloodstream."

—Herschell Gordon Lewis

By 1972, H.G. Lewis could see the writing on the wall; the major film studios were now moving into the exploitation market, squeezing out the outlaw filmmakers. "When the major companies began to ask themselves how long this had been going on, they invaded that turf with the kind of equipment and effects that made it impossible for the independents to compete," Lewis explains. "The playing time was diminishing. If a theater could play one of my movies, which had Joe Glutz in it, or a Sam Peckinpah movie which had William Holden in it, which film would that theater play?"

So Lewis decided to make one last feature — fittingly, it was a gore picture — titled *The Gore Gore Girls*. This film, which featured comedian Henny Youngman, performed extremely well at the box office and appeared to be an appropriate bookend to a successful career as a motion picture director for Lewis.

Herschell Gordon Lewis on the set of his film *The Gore Gore Girls*.

I thought *The Gore Gore Girls* was going to be the last movie I ever made. I was somewhat diffident about making the movie at all. After all, this was when the major motion picture companies had begun making the same kinds of movies that I made, except they made them with a budget, a cast, and with distribution agreements. The exhibitors were now saying, "We're not going to devote any more weeks a year to your independent movie when we can get the same kind of movie from a company with other movies behind it." They were squeezing me out. So I said, "Okay, I'll make one more and then I'll be done." And that movie became *The Gore Gore Girls*, which we we shot in Chicago.

The script for the movie was written by a fellow named Alan J. Dachman, who was the son of Bob Dachman, a friend of mine from the Variety Club in Chicago. The Variety Club was then essential to make movies because it was a national organization of theater owners with various chapters around the country. I looked at Alan's script and said, "Yeah, we can make this." It was going to require a certain amount of doctoring — you might call it "meddling," which was the nature of what I did. Not everyone agreed with my philosophy of filmmaking, but at the time, every movie I made got played. And lots of people making movies were unable to make such a claim. I bought Alan Dachman's script, and he was part of the crew when we shot it.

Right before we were about to start filming, Bob Dachman asked me, "Do you know the comedian, Henny Youngman?" I said no, I didn't know him, although I certainly knew of him. Bob said, "He's a personal friend, and he's going to be in town. Why don't you put him in your movie?" I said, "Can I afford Henny Youngman?" And Bob said, "Through me, you absolutely can afford him." I then made a deal to film Henny Youngman for one day; it was a Sunday. The deal was most favorable to me in terms of dollars. He had nothing to do that day, so whatever we paid him was extra. He was going to be in a film, and we guaranteed him a full-screen credit, which is part of the child psychology a filmmaker uses with actors anyway. And you know what? Until the day he died, Henny Youngman denied being in *The Gore Gore Girls*! It reminds me of the old Charles Addams cartoon where there is a witness in courtroom, and a huge elephant is standing there. And the man says, "What elephant?" How can you deny being in a movie that has got you all over the place? It's not as though he was only in one scene. His scenes were peppered throughout the movie. The main problem I had with Henny Youngman was the speed of his delivery. He talked so fast that it was almost impossible to decipher his words. Finally I told him, "Henny, I'm going to have to put English subtitles under your words." Once he understood what I was talking about, which obviously he hadn't prior to this, he slowed 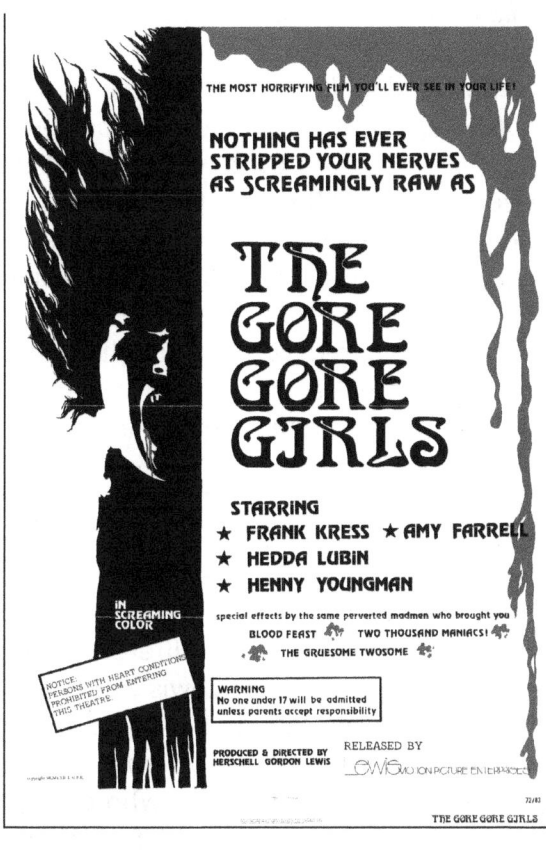 down and we had no further troubles with him. He was most cooperative in the shooting of the movie.

In this film, I used my usual stock company of actors. Ray Sager played the role of a bartender in between working on the crew. Alex Ameripoor plays a part called Grout — a lunatic who goes around smashing grapefruit with his fists. And again, Alex was on the crew. It wasn't the least bit unusual for us to have someone who was both crew and cast on the same picture. It just made sense; especially in the let's-all-pitch-in kind of movies I was making. No one had any one position, including myself.

When the movie screened, I ran it with another movie I owned. This was not a movie that I made. I purchased it through Guffanti Film Laboratory in New York. The producers had made this movie, then titled *Vortex*, and had run out of money. The lab then kept the film on a lien. Eventually, after a certain amount of time, the lab went to court and got a court order awarding them ownership of the film. After purchasing *Vortex*, I retitled it *Stick It in Your Ear*. The film, as I remember it, was a black-and-white New York film that made little sense. But I didn't care — I just needed a movie to run with *The Gore Gore Girls*, and I wasn't about to go out and shoot one. Running it alongside *The Gore Gore Girls* had two positive effects: 1) it gave me a complete double feature so the theater couldn't cheat me out of my percentage, and 2) it made *The Gore Gore Girls* look good in contrast.

The Gore Gore Girls was really a title which proved to be a miracle of effectiveness. At the time, there was a popular phrase "go-go girls." Everyone knew what go-go girls were. Well, we called them Gore Gore Girls. Once again, there were no four-letter words in this film, and it had minimal nudity. I think there were one or two scenes in which we showed breasts. This could not be considered a breakthrough film for that, but it was a breakthrough in that it was the first movie of this type with a sense of humor. I think this may be a factor in why *The Gore Gore Girls* has been as successful as it has been.

Lewis had already been retired from the movie business for 28 years when he was approached by would-be filmmakers Jacky Lee Morgan and W. Boyd Ford about making a sequel to *Blood Feast*. The two men were in town working in different capacities on Larry Clark's film *Bully*, and both were fans of Lewis' original 1963 film. Eventually a deal was worked out regarding the rights to the film, and Lewis was hired to direct *Blood Feast 2: All U Can Eat*. Lewis was then reunited with his old partner David F. Friedman, who came on board to produce the film.

Reviewer Mike Sutton of *The Digital Fix* observes: "The special effects in *Blood Feast 2* are notable for being considerably better than the ones in earlier Lewis gore extravaganzas, where most of the gore was cooked up on the cheap — the famous example being the scene in *The Gore Gore Girls* where a girl's nipples bleed chocolate milk after being cut off with scissors. The effects in this latest opus vary from the functional . . . to the exceptionally good. From the opening deaths of two tramps, one of whom removes his own intestines, to the hilariously over-the-top orgy of violence at the wedding which climaxes the film, fans of gore will be in hog heaven."

After *The Gore Gore Girls*, I thought my career in the movie industry was finished. I had another career, which was beginning to pay very, very well and on a much more stable basis. As I've often pointed out, in the movie industry I achieved some level of notoriety, whereas in the direct response marketing world I've achieved a certain amount of fame. I've written a whole bunch of books, and I'm called on to speak at very august events all over the world, on every continent. And until the Internet exposed me, the two worlds did not collide. So I wasn't really unhappy. I thought I'd had a good run.

But then Jimmy Maslon, who became my architect of destiny, rediscovered this stuff. He really has spent his entire career buying up my old movies and re-exploiting them. And when he began to re-release these movies — first on videocassette, then on DVD, with the occasional theatrical screening — the phone began to ring. It wasn't that easy then, because anyone can reach me. And there you'd have thought I'd been in the witness protection program. People didn't know if I lived in Illinois or Florida or Paducah, Kentucky. "How do you get a hold of this guy?" But they either tracked me down, or they called Jimmy, who knew where I was. And I began receiving communications saying, "Let's make *Blood Feast 2*."

Now obviously to make *Blood Feast 2* people had to negotiate with Jimmy Maslon. And most of the people who called had never heard of Jimmy Maslon. They called believing I still had the rights to *Blood Feast*, which I did not; nor did Dave Friedman. The calls and letters started coming in at a rate which made me ask, "What is happening here? What is the cause of this renaissance?" So I established what I regarded as the perfect foil; I said, "Put your deal together, and call me." And that got rid of them. They either wanted to get their names in *Variety*, or they just had a wild idea, or they weren't in the movie business at all.

Then, finally, I received a call one day. The fellow said, "My name is Jacky Lee Morgan. I'm the line producer on a movie called *Bully*, which we're shooting here in Fort Lauderdale. I'd like to have dinner with you and discuss the possibility of making *Blood Feast 2*." Well, that struck home because everything he said told me that he was really in the business and was not just some dilettante. He was quite specific in what he was talking about. So we made a deal to have dinner, and I left there saying, "I don't know what's going to happen." I referred him to Jimmy Maslon. And Jimmy called me on the phone one day and said, "This fellow really seems serious. What do you know about him?" I said, "I know nothing about him other than that he wants to make *Blood Feast 2*."

The next thing I hear, Jacky Morgan has made a deal. He had a friend named W. Boyd Ford who had written a script, and he sent me the script in the mail. I looked at that script and I didn't know what to think. I didn't think it was in the spirit of *Blood Feast*. Well, maybe it was in the spirit of the original *Blood Feast*, but the world had come quite a distance since we had shot that primitive effort. So I sent him back a note, saying to myself, "Why are you even bothering?" But I did bother, and in my note I made some suggestions for plotlines that were not in Boyd Ford's script. About three weeks later, I got another script in the mail — with most of my suggestions incorporated. And I said, "Great heavens, this man is going to make this movie!"

Jacky and I negotiated an agreement. He lived in a suburb of New Orleans, and he wanted to shoot the movie there. Honestly, I didn't care if he wanted to shoot it on the planet Mars, because it meant getting back into harness. As much as I had said I was through — probably in an effort to convince myself — I really love directing. If the next call I receive on this telephone is someone saying, "I'm ready to go on *Mr. Bruce and the Gore Machine*," I'll say, "I can't shoot it before eight o'clock tonight."

I made a deal to direct that picture. There were several problems pertaining to *Blood Feast 2*. Number one, Jackie already had his crew together when I showed up. So, I didn't have much to do with the crew. Yes, it put me as director, for the first time ever, in an actual director's chair. I even had an assistant director. He was a rather pompous young man. I was not allowed to yell, "roll sound" or "cut!" I would almost whisper it to my assistant director, who then would yell out "roll sound" or "cut!" It wasn't my crew, and obviously it wasn't my script. Sure, there were changes in there that I felt were logical, but it was not the script I would have used.

The assistant cameraman they had could not load that Panavision camera. A Panavision camera has a Mitchell movement, and if ever there was anyone on this planet who knew who to load a Mitchell camera, it was I. I have loaded Mitchell cameras in every condition you can imagine. I kept saying, "Jacky, let me load the doggone camera." And he would say, "No, no, no. You're the director. You can't do that." Also, the cameraman thought he was shooting *Ben-Hur*. He was selecting camera angles I felt were slowing down the production for no reason, angles that not only would add nothing to the effectiveness but would have someone sitting in a seat saying, "What is that?" But there again I was easy to overrule because this was not my picture. I was a hired hand. And I can't complain, because I got paid.

And most significant, it wasn't my cast. He cast it with actors from around New Orleans, most of whom were totally competent; including, by the way, Jackie's wife, Melissa, who did a great job.

Jacky was not fond of Joe Castro, whom he had hired to do the effects. The two of them were embattled throughout this movie. I felt that Joe Castro did a very creditable job, but again it was not mine to make or break. But the dissension on the set was most unusual for a movie I was involved with. We never had arguments on our sets. But on this one, there were arguments.

Another problem I had with the film was that I had nothing to do with distribution. I put together a trailer that I thought was going to sell that movie, and they didn't use it. They also made a deal with Media Blasters as the principal distributor, a deal I was unhappy with. I never did own one frame of that movie. I got paid to direct that picture, and I was out. So from the viewpoint of finance, I had nothing to lose. However, from the viewpoint of image, to have a movie like that just sit was very bothersome.

After shooting *Blood Feast 2: All U Can Eat*, Lewis found himself aching to return to the director's seat. He wrote a screenplay, which he titled *Grim Fairy Tales*. The script then sat on the shelf collecting dust for the next five years. "I was ready to go whenever someone said the word 'go,' " Lewis recalls.

Then, through a twist of fate, Lewis' two professional lives — exploitation film director and direct marketing expert — collided. He had given speeches on writing copy for a company called American Writers and Artists for many years. One day the company's owner, Mark Ford, asked him, "Didn't you used to be in the movie business?" Lewis said yes, and Ford then asked to see what he was working on at the time. Lewis e-mailed him a copy of the script. Two days later Ford called and said, "I'm ready when you are."

And the rest is history. The film, which Lewis retitled *The Uh! Oh! Show*, would be one of the finest of his long and storied career.

The original title of *The Uh! Oh! Show* was *Grim Fairy Tales*. The reason I ultimately changed the title halfway through production was because people in various film and trade magazines were asking me, "Is this a live-action version of the original Grimm Brothers' fairy tales?" I said, "No, it's just a title. There's only one 'm' in my 'Grim,' and there are two m's in Grimm Brothers." It eventually reached a point where enough people had asked the question that I think others, who didn't ask, just assumed.

It was the first picture I ever shot totally digitally, and I'm pleased with the way it turned out. We shot it with the new RED camera — the latest technological advancement. These are gigantic cameras. People think of digital as being somebody holding a little handheld camera. Not these; these were big professional cameras. The quality on screen — a theatrical screen — is superior, in my opinion, to film. I believe 35mm color film is going to be obsolete in regards to the making of movies in the next decade. It's just too easy and cost effective to shoot them digitally.

We shot *The Uh! Oh! Show* in the Tampa Bay area — St. Petersburg and Clearwater. The quality of the acting in the film is exactly what I wanted. I could not have had better cooperation under any circumstances. The cast and crew were as talented and as cooperative as I've ever worked with. It was a genuine pleasure to shoot that movie.

The only thing I'm unhappy with regarding *The Uh! Oh! Show*, so far — and as of this comment it's just now going into release — is the distribution deal the producer made. Again, I was under a contract. I wrote it and I directed it, but I had absolutely nothing to do with distribution. That will teach me! My opinion is that the deal they made was not the kind of distribution this picture deserved.

But all in all, I was extremely pleased with the finished product. In my opinion, *The Uh! Oh! Show* is one of the more polished of this type of film ever made.

INDEX

Abel, Robert 12-13
Aberman, Larry 42, 43, 92
The Adventures of Lucky Pierre 9, 18-23, 25, 73
Allen, Rusty 25, 26, 28
Alley Tramp 101-102
American International Pictures 103, 105, 106
American Writers and Artists 135
Ameripoor, Alex 104, 126, 131
Ames, Julie 101
Anger, Kenneth 79
Arkoff, Sam 103, 105
Arnold, Mal 40, 46, 48, 51
Arums, Mudite 84
Baker, Jack 80, 81
Bartlett, Dick 36, 37
Bartlett, Robert 36
Beasley, Jack 126
Bedell, Rodney 99, 106
Bee, Robbie 37
Behn, Noel 14
Bell, Bare and Beautiful 43-46
Bell, Virginia 43, 44
Ben-Hur 32, 134
Berg, Hal 78, 79, 80
Berg, Jo Ann 78, 79
Black, Karen 10, 13, 14, 40
Black Love 122, 123-125
Blank, Taalkius "Talky" 58, 67, 68, 82, 128
Blast-Off Girls 83, 87-89, 93
Blight, David 79
Blood Feast 5, 7, 26, 40, 43, 46, 47-56, 60, 63, 66, 67, 83, 97, 105, 132, 133
Blood Feast 2: All U Can Eat 132-135
Boeing, Boeing 39
Bogart, Humphrey 126
Boin-n-g! 35-39
Born Losers 106
Boulton, Lyn 48
Brigadoon 56
Brinkman, Dick 73
Buckalew, Bethel "Buck" 117, 122
Bully 132, 133
Camp, Walter 113
The Candidate 127
Carnival Story 10
The Carol Burnett Show 15
Cashiers du Cinemart 7
Castro, Joe 135
Champion, Paul 59
Chaplin, Charles 11, 12
Chudnow, Byron 112

Chudnow, David 85, 111, 112
Chudnow, Rosamund 112
Cinema Wasteland 7
Clark, Bonnie 113
Clark, Larry 132
Cler, Judy 119, 120
Collodi, Roy 53
Color Me Blood Red 61-64, 66, 110
Connell, Betty 103
Conway, Dan 87
Corman, Roger 97
The Curious Adventures of Mr. Wonderbird 78
Curry, Christopher Wayne 5-6, 47, 118
Curtin, Jack 19, 20, 21
Curtis, Tony 39
D'Hondt, Danica 16
Dachman, Alan J. 130-131
The Daily Oklahoman 125
"Dang Me" 128
Daughter of the Sun 25-28
Davis, Elizabeth 98
Davis, Jr., Sammy 94
De Niro, Robert 40
Depp, Johnny 40
The Digital Fix 132
Doctor Gore 74
Dominant Pictures of the Carolinas 66
Donovan, Dixie 121
Dowd, Kevin 30, 113
Dowd, Tom 22, 28-29, 30, 31, 32, 33, 39, 43, 45, 101, 102, 113, 114, 116, 117
Downe, Allison-Louise 29, 37, 47, 49, 86, 101, 102, 116
Drake, Larry 125, 127
DVD Drive-In 94
The Ecstasies of Women 109, 113-114
Erman, Bill 14
Essanay Studios 11
An Eye for an Eye 77-78
Falbo, Billy 18, 20, 23
Flynn, Errol 62
Ford, Mark 135
Ford, W. Boyd 132, 134
Fred Niles Film Studio 11, 16
Friedman, David 1, 9, 12, 14, 15, 17, 18, 19, 20, 22, 23, 25, 26, 28, 29, 31, 32, 35, 39, 43, 44, 48, 50, 51, 52, 54, 56, 61, 63, 64, 65, 66, 67, 110, 132
The Giant Behemoth 13
The Giant Spider Invasion 70
Gilbreth, Jack 105

The Girl, the Body and the Pill 91-93
Girls, Guns and Ghouls 106
Glen or Glenda 110
Glore, Charles 65, 68
Goldilocks and the Three Bares 7, 31-33
Gone with the Wind 91
Gordon, Al 46
Gordone, Paul 101
The Gore Gore Girls 40, 129-132, 133
Graham, Herb 13
Green, Jerome 25, 26-28, 29, 48, 61
Griffith, Leroy 43, 44, 45
The Gruesome Twosome 97-99
Guffanti Film Laboratory 132
Gulliver's Travels 127
Gyenes, Agi 104, 106
Hall, Scott 48, 53, 61
A Hard Day's Night 87
Harlow, Jean 42
Harris, Bill 61
Hawn, Goldie 121
Hefner, Hugh 14, 15, 52
Hitchcock, Alfred 5
Hite, Henry 72
Hodges, Joy 44
Hogue, Jeff 74
Hoffman, Harry 68
Holden, William 129
Holt, Tim 40, 125, 126-127
Horrorwitz, Brian 7
"How Dry I Am" 51
How to Make a Doll 85, 111-112
Hunter, Paul 78
Hurkos, Peter 84, 109, 110
Hurlew Productions 83
Hurley, James 83, 84-85, 109, 110, 111
Huston, Walter 126
The Incredible Dobermans 112
International Alliance of Theatrical Stage Employees 12, 88-89
Jackson, Eli 43, 44, 45
Jimmy the Boy Wonder 77, 78-80
Johnson, Bill 28, 35, 36, 37
Joseph, Erwin 12, 14, 17
Just for the Hell of It 85, 101, 106-107
Kahn, Alan 118-119
Kansas Censor Board 55
Kerr, Harry 65, 66, 67, 68, 69, 70, 74
Kerwin, Bill 15, 16, 35, 36, 39, 40-42, 44, 47, 58, 77, 79, 86, 106
Kiddie Matinee 79
The King and I 96

King, Claude 127, 128
"King of the Road" 128
Kohlberg, Stan 35, 36, 55, 62, 63, 109, 110, 111, 124
Korman, Harvey 15, 40
L.A. Law 127
Lake, Veronica 106-107
Laughlin, Tom 106
LeCompte, Jo Ann 14
Lewis and Martin Films 11, 19, 37
Lewis, Jerry 11
Lewis, Robert 99
Linda and Abilene 113, 115-17
Living Venus 9, 14-18, 40, 85
Logay, Don 86
Lucky Pierre Enterprises 18
Lugosi, Boris 106
The Magic Land of Mother Goose 80-82
Man of the Year 127
Manson, Charles 115, 116
March, Fredric 107
Mark, Tony 121
Marlow, Rex 31-32, 33
Martell, Chris 99
Martin, Dean 11
Mashbitz, George 88
Mason, Connie 48, 50, 51, 52, 56, 58-59
Maslon, Jimmy 22, 59, 70, 74, 78, 80, 133
Matt, Dennis 114
Matt, Sharon 113-114, 116
Maxim, Joey 31, 32, 33
Mayflower Pictures 97, 118, 121
McGinn, Jim 15, 85
Media Blasters 135
Metro-Goldwyn-Mayer 103
Meyer, Russ 22, 105
Mid-Continent Films 11, 17
Miller, Roger 128
Miss Nymphet's Zap-In 121-122, 124
Modern Film Distributors 9, 11-12, 17, 18, 19
Mom and Dad 74
Monster-A-Go-Go 70-74
Moonshine Mountain 65-70, 73, 86, 112, 125
Moore, Ben 67, 86
Morgan, Jacky Lee 132, 133, 134
Morgan, Melissa 135
Motion Picture Association of America 122
Movie Musings and Grumblings 110
Murray, K. Gordon 30, 37
"My Pappy Built a Still" 68
The National Insider 117
Nature's Playmates 28-31

Neumann, Kurt 10
Niles, Fred 12, 14
Noble, Nancy Lee 92, 103, 106
Noe, Gaspar 7
Nude on the Moon 80
Oas-Heim, Gordon 61-62, 68, 69
Olsen, Astrid 50, 51
Palmer, Randy 77
Paramount 103
Patterson, Pat 74
Peckinpah, Sam 129
Playboy 14, 15, 48, 50
The Prime Time 9-14, 15, 16, 17
"The Prime Time" (song) 10
The Projection Booth 7
The Psychic 83, 85, 109-111
Psycho 5
Ratay, Wayne 119
Rebane, Bill 70, 71, 72, 73, 74
Red Dust 42
Redford, Robert 43, 127
Reich, Sidney 36, 62, 64, 110
Reservoir Dogs 48
Riddle, Ronna 128
"The Rime of the Ancient Mariner" 17
Roberts, Luanne 121
Rolnick, Ione 86
Ross, Eddie 23
Roth, Eli 7
Rotolo, Joanne 37
Rowan and Martin's Laugh-In 121
Sack, Al 19, 20
Sager, Ray 87, 106, 118, 119, 128
Sanders, Harlan 87
Sandy, Fred 97, 102, 103, 106, 118, 119, 121
Santo, Vincent 59
Sassy Sue 117
Schmidhofer, Martin 11, 37-38
Schwartz, Abbott 78
Screen Actors Guild 107
Scum of the Earth 6, 7, 39-43
Shaft 123
Shakespeare, William 26
She-Devils on Wheels 102-106
Sin, Suffer and Repent 74-75
Sinatra, Frank 94
Sinclair, Sandy 48
Sindelar, Dave 110
Sinise, Bob 64
Sinise, Gary 64
Smith, Bob 123, 124

Something Weird 83-85
Sonney, Dan 64
Sophocles 19
Sousa, John Philip 49
"The South's Gonna Rise Again" 59
Southern Comfort 117
Stanford, Donald "Dok" 93, 94
Stick It in Your Ear 132
Strauss, Johan 49
Strauss, Robert 120
Suburban Roulette 85-87
Sutton, Mike 132
Sweet Sweetback's Baadasssss Song 123
Swift, Jonathan 127
A Taste of Blood (film) 91, 93-97
A Taste of Blood: The Films of Herschell Gordon Lewis (book) 47, 118
"Teenage Tiger" 10
This Stuff'll Kill Ya! 40, 123, 125-27
Thunder Road 65
Tobacco Rooty 117
Trash Palace 7
The Treasure of the Sierra Madre 40, 125, 126
Turner Classic Movies 73
Twentieth Century-Fox 29
Two Thousand Maniacs! 36, 54, 56-60, 61, 62, 63, 66, 67, 86, 89, 102, 110, 125
Tyrell, Tom 87
The Uh! Oh! Show 7, 135-136
United Film and Recording 14, 16, 18, 21, 71
Variety 133
Variety Club 130
Wagner, Christie 103
Weisenborn, Gordon 11, 12, 13-14
Wellington, Larry 21, 79
Wells, Gretchen 99
White, Mike 7
White, Steve 101, 106
Whitman, Walt 47
The Wild Bunch 48
Wilkinson, Elizabeth 86
Williams, Robin 127
Wishman, Doris 80
Witherspoon, Reese 52
"Wolverton Mountain" 128
Wood, Ed 110
The Wizard of Gore 118-120
The Wizard of Oz 79
Year of the Yahoo! 88, 127-128
"You Are My Sunshine" 87
Youngman, Henny 40, 129, 131

www.ingramcontent.com/pod-product-compliance
Lightning Source LLC
Chambersburg PA
CBHW070919160426
43193CB00011B/1524